DEFRIENDED

Deena,

One of my first NY friends + a woman I admire for her strength + conviction. All the best in life & love!

♡ Christina

For Mom, Dad and Anthony...

One word.

DEFRIEND (v.)- the act of removing someone from your friends list on any social network; the act of ending a friendship with someone either on a social network or in the online world.

DEFRIENDED:
A Guide to Breaking Up and Shaping Up

by
Christina Morelli

"A friend took me to the most amazing place the other day. It's called the Augusteum. Octavian Augustus built it to house his remains. When the barbarians came they trashed it a long with everything else. The great Augustus, Rome's first true great emperor. How could he have imagined that Rome, the whole world as far as he was concerned, would be in ruins. It's one of the quietest, loneliest places in Rome. The city has grown up around it over the centuries. It feels like a precious wound, a heartbreak you won't let go of because it hurts too good. We all want things to stay the same. Settle for living in misery because we're afraid of change, of things crumbling to ruins. Then I looked at around to this place, at the chaos it has endured — the way it has been adapted, burned, pillaged and found a way to build itself back up again. And I was reassured, maybe my life hasn't been so chaotic, it's just the world that is, and the real trap is getting attached to any of it. Ruin is a gift. Ruin is the road to transformation."

-Elizabeth Gilbert, *Eat, Pray, Love*

Table of Contents

Foreword

We all have a voice that lives inside our head. Some of us have more than one. Mine is a little fat girl. Let's call her Molly.

That voice is the driving force behind almost every bad decision and self-destructive tendency you'll ever experience in your life. She's made excuses for why you gained twenty-five pounds in college. She's the asshole who made you believe that you could handle "just one last time" with your ex. She's the scapegoat for all those nights you got dressed, looked in a mirror, and crawled back into bed in a deep depression over your perceived inadequacies that led to the perfect storm of your late twenties. Or maybe that's just mine. Either way, that stops today.

That voice is a bitch. And before you can ever understand how to "defriend" those toxic relationships, you'll have to learn how to delete her. This book is the first step you'll take in telling your "Molly" to take a hike and start owning up to your actions, your decisions, and your life.

YOU are in control. In the next eight chapters, you will learn how to pick yourself up from the lowest situations, the greatest heartbreaks, the "rock bottoms," and become the amazing person that you were, are, and always will be. You will learn to recognize and change the patterns that have sabotaged your happiness time and time again. You're moving in a forward direction now, entering the next stage of this crazy, wild ride we call life... battle wounds in tow.

You're going to be okay. Don't let any other voice tell you otherwise.

PART I: BREAKING UP

DE **4** FRIENDED

Chapter One

Who The Hell Are You?

"Faith is taking the first step even when you don't see the whole staircase." ~Martin Luther King, Jr.

Despite being a trained dancer and relatively active child, my weight was something I battled with my whole life. When I entered college and was no longer dancing full-time, the pounds crept on like a cold you can't shake no matter how many doses of Emergen-C you consume. The Freshman 15 turned into the Sophomore 25, and at graduation I was almost thirty pounds heavier than I was in high school. My graduation pictures, shot at an angle that captures the monstrosity of my double chin and puffy eyes, have been locked away with the threat of painful and violent death to my parents and brother if they were ever to reveal them to someone outside of my immediate family.

For the years that followed, I struggled to lose that college weight, trying every diet fad known to man and immersing myself back into dance class despite the fact that my body no longer moved the way it used to. By 2007, four years after graduation, I was only down about ten pounds and had seemed to hit a wall. And then on one warm spring night in May, I met the guy who would prove to be the best diet ever. He shall be known as "Jack." Voldemort was already taken.

Our relationship started off slow. He was coming right out of a terrible break up and I had been single for quite some time and wasn't looking to dive into anything serious. Soon after we started seeing each other, I was hooked, and when he put the brakes on things just a few months after dating, I was devastated. The weeks that followed his sudden retraction left me without an appetite, which often happens when you get dumped. The pounds started to drop off quickly; though I'm sure half of it was water weight coming out in the form of tears. I gave myself a week to be sad, engaging in the typical "what's wrong with me/I must not be pretty/skinny/hot enough" mentality, and before I could delete his number from my phone, he was texting me "I miss you." So ended Round One of the never-ending break up.

Round Two was a little more intense, as fall had approached and the holiday season was settling in. We spent more time together as a "couple" and after he agreed to come to the city with my family to celebrate our annual holiday brunch and a Broadway show, I was convinced this was the real deal. When we returned home from that evening, I knew something was wrong. He was distant, standoffish, and clearly uncomfortable to be around me just hours after leaving the city, so I questioned him.

One week later, on Christmas Eve, I received an e-mail that he was breaking up with me, and would prefer if our contact were limited to writing because he couldn't handle talking to me. Merry fucking Christmas.

For two and half years after that e-mail, we danced around this dysfunctional relationship, struggling with what could only be described as destructive codependency, constantly sabotaging every chance at happiness. We would stop speaking for weeks, sometimes even months, only to see each other again and fall prey to the toxic chemistry that fueled the emotional rollercoaster. The problem was, we were both on it for different reasons.

In the meantime, I was an emotional wreck. Through the wonders of Facebook, one month after we broke up, I discovered that he had already started hooking up with someone else. Each time she would post a new picture of the two of them getting cozy at some party, I would lose my appetite for days. Over the years, the number of women he was involved with grew, and as we continued to try and fail at being friends, my heart would break more and more. The pattern was always the same: after the wave of sadness would pass, I'd take my frustrations out on the dance floor, on the pavement, up my Pilates routine, or engage in basically any form of physical activity that would help my body feel strong even though my heart was fragile and weak. Just as I was starting to feel confident again, he would show up with a new girl, leaving me to scrutinize, compare, and beat myself up for not being enough for him. I convinced myself that the better I looked, the better chance I had of winning him back, so I set forth to be as hot and desirable as possible. For the record, this made absolutely zero difference in why he was/wasn't attracted to me.

I lost a total of twenty pounds since the day we met, and for the first time in my entire life, kept it off. Of course, there was the five pound fluctuation that usually reared its ugly head around Christmas (cookies) and Easter (jelly beans), but once I learned what my triggers were, it became easier to get back on track.

During that period of time many other aspects of my life changed. I closed the Philadelphia-based business I had started at twenty-three years old and made the big move to New York City to pursue several new careers and discover the joys and pitfalls of being broke and a bit scattered for awhile. This "new life" led to a variety of beautiful friendships, some mortifying yet memorable experiences, a brief drinking problem, and an interesting, twisted path into discovering where my talents also lie. I finally took some time off to travel and do volunteer work, which unlocked a new, healthier addiction, and above all... I grew up.

In the past few years, I've lived in multiple sublets with complete strangers, traded dog-sitting for housing, taught myself photography, worked at a hair salon, ran a half marathon, got my first tattoo, started a new business, a website, and several books, and most importantly, learned what it's like to truly be alone. There were moments when I felt so weak I could not get out of bed for days, and there were times when I was fueled with so much anger that I put myself in positions that were downright embarrassing, but every single thing that happened since that initial break up, for better or worse, carved the path of my life today.

The most fascinating part of the whole experience was that it took my heartbreak for me to finally realize that my weight issues were mainly psychological and more in my control than I realized. I attempted to strip everything down and looked at myself, my decisions, and my actions realistically, and decided to figure out the truth behind what happened. Then I looked at my body, honestly. I thought about what sort of changes and physical transformations had occurred since the day we met, and how differently I viewed myself, my approach to exercise, and my eating habits.

The conclusion? The patterns and habits that kept me from losing weight were the same self-destructive tendencies that kept me from getting over my ex. In both cases, I would sabotage my efforts regularly, taking months to recover from a slip up instead of forgiving myself for a mistake and returning to a healthy state of mind. In both cases, I blamed outside circumstances, whether it was genetics, friends, or other women for my inability to stay in control. In both cases, I had so little confidence in my strengths and in myself that I gave into every temptation as if I was trying to prove I wasn't strong enough to change. This major epiphany took years of analyzing, scrutinizing, and reflecting before I came to terms with a lot of it, and to be honest in the end, it turned out to be easier to shed my weight than to shed my fucked up love life. Part of that was because while I could avoid the candy aisle at the grocery store, I could not avoid him at our weekly hangout with whatever woman happened to be by his side that week.

Regardless, my addiction to both food and love needed to be waned. So, after years of trial-and-error, I finally recognized four important steps to recovering, rebuilding, and reshaping your life. This level of self-awareness can lead to some seriously frightening revelations, so I hope you're ready. Here are my little gems of wisdom and enlightenment, you lucky little bastards. I hope that my multiple failures and experiences will help you shave even just a few weeks off your recovery process and leave you with a sense of empowerment moving forward.

This guide is a "rehab" program of sorts; one that's meant to provide guidance, suggestions, comfort, and a few laughs during a period of your life when you feel everything has fallen apart. It's a compilation of personal experience, advice from professionals, research, and insight by people just like you and I to inspire you to be the brilliant, gorgeous, and talented person you lost sight of along the way. For the record, this is not a FDA-tested, doctor-approved weight loss method... AKA "diet." I don't believe in that word anymore, especially after being on one for most of my life. Don't call Dr. Oz and brag about how you lost twenty pounds on this great new "break up diet"... but if you want, feel free to flaunt it in front of your ex that he blew it, big time. Trust me, he'll see it on Facebook either way.

Take away what you need from it, and leave the rest for someone else. The sole purpose of this book is to remind you that you're not alone. We've all dated that one asshole (some of us have dated multiple assholes) and if you were lucky enough to dodge the douchebag bullet, then stop gloating for a minute and share this with your poor best friend who wants to slit her wrists every time you and your significant other call each other "babe," make out in public, and show up in coordinating outfits.

Each individual follows a different path and a different journey, and how we heal and recover makes us unique and special in our own way. The fact that you are even reading this indicates that you are ready to make some changes, which is always the first step in any recovery plan.

I first finished this book in April 2011, just short of four years from when Jack and I first met. After it was completed, I put it away... for a YEAR. Didn't read it. Didn't open it. It sat in my saved documents on lockdown. Part of the reason was because I was worried what other people would think. In retrospect, I think it's pretty obvious EVERYONE knew how badly he had hurt and affected me. I figured that part out when the last crop of astronauts rotating through space over NYC sent me a text that said "Are you okay?" Another reason was that I didn't want to boost HIS ego by letting him know in a public medium how much the past few years wrecked me. It was a sign of weakness, and I am a strong, independent woman, dammit! "I won't give him the satisfaction of writing a book inspired by our relationship!" I thought. Well, that's just stupid. Look at Adele. I'm pretty sure she doesn't care that her ex knows that 21 was inspired by him. I'm also pretty sure Adele had the last laugh. Oh and Adele, if you're reading this, call me. I'm thinking movie soundtrack. We should chat.

I digress. When I came back to this book almost exactly one year later, I had a saddening, embarrassing and MAJOR realization—I had not taken my own advice. Idiot. Here I was, all, "Find yourself, let go, be beautiful and wonderful and strong," and in the meantime I was still sending him angry, psycho text messages and trying to be his damn friend. And as I approached the five year anniversary of my attempt to exorcise myself one last time of burdening insecurities, fears, and self-loathing that accumulated over thirty years of eating disorders and a shitty love life, I added a final chapter to this book, "One Year Later." This chapter serves as the truthful epilogue to what it's really like to let go of your past, live in the present, and rediscover yourself. And this time, I'm not fucking around.

Welcome to your first step, DEFRIENDED: a four-stage guide to breaking up and shaping up to finding peace, health, happiness, truth and most importantly, finding YOU.

*And to delete your ex from your Facebook page, once and for all.

Chapter Two:

Me. Naked.

"The definition of insanity is doing the same thing over and over again and expecting different results." ~Albert Einstein

I was a late bloomer. As a kid, I was often made fun of for my weight—"Mean Girls" style—and it held me back from ever feeling really confident or attractive around boys. I met my first boyfriend when I was sixteen, but prior to him, all I had really done was kiss a guy, and maybe a little waist-up action. Ron was one year older than me and a total schmoozer. He had a girlfriend at the time we met and gallantly broke up with her for me after seeing my sweet dance moves at auditions for the school musical. Welcome to High School 101, where we like to make every situation as dramatic as an episode of GLEE. After Ron dumped his girlfriend, he had to keep me a "secret" because he didn't want any of their friends to tell her that he had met someone new. So when we were in school, there was to be no hand holding in the hallways and no kissing near the lockers. Scandalous.

Despite Ron's proven track record with infidelity and my non-existent love life prior to him, he was always convinced I was cheating on him. I couldn't figure out how to handle HIM at the time—much less a guy on the side—so I don't know where he got the idea that I had this frat house full of boys that I would sneak off to and have meaningless sex with, but he had his eyes (and his friends' eyes) on me at all times. I haven't liked being controlled or told what to do since I took my first breath, so Ron's oppressive ways did not fly well with me. The more I resisted his overbearing "love," the more frustrated he became. He got back at me by dumping my ass and cheating on me with one of my friends. That was my first taste at heartbreak. Yes, I'd had years of unrequited love prior to that, but there's a certain swift punch to the gut when you show up at your ex-boyfriend's house to talk two days after he dumps you and you're greeted at the door by your friend wearing his clothes. Needless to say, I looked great in a bikini that summer.

I'll give you two guesses to figure out what I did next. (If you read the first chapter closely, you should know by now what a schmuck I am with men and can probably figure it out in one guess). Was your answer, "Take the cheating, lying bastard back and go on to lose your virginity to him?" If so, you would be correct.

We dated for a few years after that, on and off, and that relationship finally ended for good my sophomore year of college. This coincided with the beginning of an unfortunate weight gain that I liked to blame on the Pill but I'm pretty sure was related to the rows of Ritz crackers and peanut butter I would mindlessly eat while my college friends went out and had random sex with drunk guys. Here is something I must point out though — Ron NEVER had any issues with my body. He loved it, actually. No man I ever slept with criticized or showed any indication that they would change any part of me. Except maybe my mouth. (Because I'm constantly speaking my mind, that is. Get your mind out of the gutter.)

The second close relationship I developed with a man was in college. James and I met our junior year during a semester abroad, and couldn't stand each other at first. We fought much like Harry and Sally (as in "When Harry Met Sally," a movie that anyone with a pulse should know, RIP Norah Ephron). Our relationship resembled Harry and Sally only if Harry had actually been a closeted gay man. Oops. I just spoiled the end to this fairytale.

James had a snarky sense of humor and loved to tell stories at other people's expenses. He was actually funny, as long as you weren't the subject of his stories, which I often was. We had one of those strange relationships where when we got along, we were best of friends, but when he turned on me, he was vicious. I later learned this was largely due in part to his heavy, burdening secret life and undisclosed sexuality, but regardless, his sarcastic jokes about my weight and running commentary pointing out every one of my insecurities was never pleasant. However, we had a rare, special connection and to this day, I'll tell you he's one of the few people I can be brutally honest with and know that I'll receive it in return. There's something refreshing about that in a world riddled with countless people with multiple personality disorder.

One of my favorite things about James was how he challenged me. Though some would find his crude jokes and constant picking to be cruel, I found them motivating. I always wanted to prove him wrong. Sometimes he crossed the line, and we had our share of knock down drag outs. But at the end of the day, he was one of the few guys in my college years that I truly let in. Maybe it was only because in the back of my head, I always had my suspicions about his sexuality. In a strange way, it made me feel safe. I would never have to worry about him judging what I looked like naked, because he had zero desire to SEE me naked. Unlike other males in my life whose lack of interest drove me straight to the gym and starvation mode, I gained a significant amount of weight during my friendship with James because I was comfortable. It was never about sex.

Our senior year, James came out of the closet. Though at the time I was the picture perfect supportive friend, a part of me really struggled. We never had a physical relationship, but I didn't want to share him and I knew that in him growing comfortable in his new lifestyle, I would lose him on some level. I was just as possessive over James as I would have been over a real boyfriend, something I recognize as extremely unhealthy and destructive now, but not at twenty-one years old. When we graduated college, he suddenly went "back in," at least to the general public. His family and friends back home didn't know he was gay, and I suppose it was easier to pretend than to go through the whole "coming out" process again. The saddest part? I BELIEVED him! I believed he really might be straight. It's scary what we accept as truth so as to not deal with reality.

For a brief period of time, I became his "beard." We constantly hung out at his house with his family, I knew his grandparents, his cousins, his group of friends at home... We went to parties and had sleepovers and I dragged him to all the things a boyfriend should have to go to even though he wasn't my boyfriend. I'm sure that if he had any questions about whether or not he was truly gay, my treating him like my fake boyfriend definitely cleared things up. One day, between me planning our apple-picking dates and asking him to yet another torturous family function, I found out he was dating someone new through a mutual friend. I felt cheated on, with the exception of the fact that we weren't dating and the person he met was a guy. Minor details. So significant relationship number two ended very similarly to significant relationship number one, except Ron's had a vagina and James' had a penis.

*For the record, James is still one of my dear friends and we've had many talks over the years over what a shitty friend he was and complete psycho I was. We still love each other and I'm confident that if I ever end up alone in a nursing home one day, he would come visit and try to beat me at Cranium. I would win.

Fast forward through four years of dating, hooking up, a few crushes that ended as unrequited love, and a proven track record to never meet someone who held my interest to the third date. Cue Kelly Clarkson's "Miss Independent." Fade out. Enter Jack.

I wasn't expecting Jack. I believe the scenario that led to our meeting was that I had asked friends and family if they knew a cute, single guy who would possibly make a great wedding date. At twenty-five, I was sick of responding without a plus one, and being awkwardly cornered by distant relatives with the question "How are you still single?" but I genuinely wasn't looking for a serious relationship. Then the Universe slapped me with a big "YOU CAN'T CONTROL EVERYTHING," and threw me into the most intense emotional, psychological, and physical hurricane my unsuspecting being had ever experienced.

In true Christina fashion, I took that hurricane, threw a microscope on it, and put that Pilates certification, dance training, diet research, and psychology degree to use in writing this book. Some might say I became obsessed. Some might be correct. Why do you think Web MD is such a successful website? Because most people want their questions answered, and immediately. What it looks like. How it happens. What the future will bring. Heartbreak can take on the form of a terminal illness if you don't treat it properly. Part II of this book outlines the main stages I went through in trying to recover, heal, and move on from 10+ years of piss poor dating judgment. If you have ever experienced a broken heart to even the smallest degree, or if you've ever cried in the dressing room and angrily thrown another pair of jeans at your mother in a rage as though she crept into your room at night and slathered cellulite on your thighs intentionally, then you will hopefully find even a small nugget of comfort as you are reading. The stages are chock full of advice, suggestions, and inspiration for setting new goals and developing a healthier lifestyle, along with humorous anecdotes to bring a smile to that pretty little face.

Chapter Three:

Letting Go

"You gain strength, courage and confidence by every experience in which you really stop to look fear in the face. You are able to say to yourself 'I have lived through this horror. I can take the next thing that comes along.' You must do the thing you think you cannot do."
~ Eleanor Roosevelt

The final piece to my personal heartbreak story is how I learned to let go. I've had to rewrite this chapter several times, because to be honest I don't have a fucking clue how to let go. I'm an emotional hoarder. My grandmother is a physical hoarder. She kept all of my grandfather's clothing in a closet for years after he passed. She has clothes and knick knacks and unopened mail strewn over her bed like a comforter. And she will often sleep on top of it, like a nest. I do the same with people. I stuff them all in my heart and my brain, and I keep them close to me long after they've sunk to the bottom of the pile. Those who may have gone awry torture my perfectionist soul every night as I try to sleep peacefully, like a random nail jutting out from beneath the clutter and mess.

Here's the thing. No one likes change, particularly change they have no control over. However, it's necessary to let go in order to live a complete life. Think of all the people whose paths you've crossed over the course of your personal history. How have they changed you? Shaped you? Defined you? Influenced you? They've done so in more ways then you probably even realize.

I spent a really long time resenting my ex. I became cynical about love, bitter toward other women, guarded around men, and downright unpleasant to be around at times. I had been rejected time and time again, and instead of telling him to fuck himself (which I did, quite often), walk away, and STAY away, I was determined to fix it. To fix him. Instead of acknowledging that I was the one who needed fixing. Clearly, the fact that I kept going back to a guy who didn't treat me well and repeatedly hurt me made me some sort of masochist, a realization which then sent me into a deeper depression. How could I let this happen to me? Our relationship, which felt quite beautiful and poetic in the beginning—he being a recently dumped tortured soul and myself being notoriously single, unattached, and unaffected by men—

spiraled into such a deep pool of resentment, hatred, and anger that it became impossible to save. I kept slamming his chest with shock paddles while the doctor repeatedly screamed "time of death" until I finally backed down in exhaustion. It was seriously tragic, and if I could go back in time and slap myself REALLY hard, I would.

I can recall a close friend of mine once saying, in the gentlest way possible, "You know, Christina, you are one of the strongest, toughest women I know when it comes to business. And yet, you get into relationships with these men and let them walk all over you." She was right. I was a tough cookie, but I had a serious addiction to bad boys who would never commit to me. And I let them get away with it.

The Silver Lining...

Everyone told me to walk away four years ago. HE told me to walk away four years ago. He knew he was bad for me, and he tried to warn me on numerous occasions. True to form of being consistently inconsistent, I didn't listen. And you know what? I'm glad I didn't. It was much more fun to challenge my sanity on a weekly basis.

Over the course of my undefined relationship and then unsuccessful attempt to be "friends," I made a lot of changes in my life. I closed my business of five years and moved to New York to start a new career, a city I have a wild love/hate relationship with that inspires me daily. I discovered a passion and talent for writing that had been previously limited to journal entries and the occasional e-mail. I made a wonderful group of friends who I can confidently say will be a part of my life forever, and I became a part of a community that I have an immense amount of respect and admiration for. I traveled to places I've always wanted to visit, lived in new countries, and experienced the joy of firsts that I would have been terrified of in my early twenties. It wasn't always beautiful and filled with rainbows and butterflies, but it was real, and it shaped me. Our relationship guided me down the path I was meant to be on, and had I walked away without looking back that miserable Christmas Eve, I would be a completely different person right now. Things DO happen for a reason—as much as you want to punch people in the face when they say that to you as you're drenching yourself in a pile of tears, snot, and self-pity.

Things did not end well between us. While I still see him regularly and we run in the same professional circles, our relationship is estranged at best and has made it difficult for me to move on. I am a person who demands answers, explanations, and reasons, and he is a person who prefers to avoid confrontation at all costs. My stubbornness had me convinced if I harassed him enough he would cave and shed some light on the situation. That worked brilliantly, as I made myself look psychotic time and time again and he pleaded with me to stop contacting him. How attractive on my behalf. My friends all tried to beat into me that I wasn't going to get closure, comparing my efforts to repeatedly continuing to touch an electric shock fence, thinking at some point it would stop zapping me. Back in the days of psychology when classical conditioning was all the rage, I would have been a nightmare of a test subject. Eventually I had to accept that I would never get my answers, and that it was time for me to start focusing on my life instead of worrying about his. I felt trapped and helpless at first, thinking my only two choices were to find a new career and new group of friends, or to spend countless nights with anxiety and sadness watching his new relationship play out, quite literally, right in front of my eyes. Let's be honest, when a notorious womanizer and commitment-phobe breaks your heart and tells you he doesn't want to be close with someone, then falls in "love" and shows up with a girlfriend not too soon after, it takes everything in your power not to haul yourself off the Brooklyn Bridge (or whatever bridge or tall building is at your disposal).

I tried everything to make something work out of it because in my mind, it took way more energy to ignore him and have no relationship whatsoever than it did to make peace with it and let go of the past. Unfortunately, we weren't on the same page with our ways of handling things, and I ultimately learned that the choice was out of my hands. Everyone told me I would move on once I met someone new, but it seemed like no matter how many guys I dated, the rejection of that one person weighed on me like a dark cloud of defeat. In fact, the few times I did meet men who were absolute sweethearts and probably would have treated me like a princess, I ran like I discovered they had gonorrhea. I didn't trust my judgment because too many times I had let someone in, only to be wrong about the kind of person they were. When he met the girl who made it easy for him to cut ME out, I did NOT handle it well. I felt replaced and taken advantage of, like I no longer served a purpose or was worth the effort.

One night over drinks, I finally confided in a friend what was holding me back from getting close to someone again. "It terrifies me, how I behaved in that relationship," I said. "I became a THAT girl—the one who called, pleaded, texted, and acted crazy and desperate because I just couldn't accept I was wrong about someone." I was all "pick me, choose me, love me" à la Grey's Anatomy Season One, and he basically said, "Nope."

The idea of getting involved with someone else who would break my heart and leave me in that state again was far worse than just being alone. To move past that kind of pain is a challenge. I learned how important it is to treat people the way you want to be treated, as cliché as that sounds. I also became extremely sensitive to not lead someone on or show an interest in a guy just for my own selfish need for attention. Many of my relationships started where I was the rebound, and it's a horrible feeling to know you're just the afterthought to the person they really loved and cared about.

On the upside, the one thing I DID maintain was my weight loss. It's been two years and I haven't fluctuated more than five pounds. My clothes all fit, shopping no longer induces tantrums and self-loathing, and aside from the week I have my period, I have definitely stayed true to all of the methods and advice I offer in the following stages. Being able to take control of that aspect of my life has been a huge stepping stone in moving on, and while the pain of that relationship still lingers, the fact that I am healthy, strong, and able to help others achieve THEIR health, fitness, and life goals makes me feel like a whole person again.

Take your time to heal. We all function and operate on different schedules and handle tragedy in different ways. Know when to push and when to hold back, when to speak and when to remain silent. Listen to your body — it will always tell you what it needs. Don't beat yourself up every time you make a mistake, whether it be texting him, eating an entire cake, or skipping a workout. Breaking any habit or addiction, whether food, drugs, or another person, takes time and reinforcement. The four stages in this guide have been designed to be repeated until you get it right. My intention is not to tell you what to do, but to offer guidance and insight I learned along the way. You're a human, not a superhero. Even Superman has his kryptonite. It's okay.

A broken heart leaves a scar, but that scar makes you a unique person, destined to be stronger, smarter, and more aware in your next relationship. I can tell you firsthand that when I meet guys now, I can instantly sniff out if I'm destined for heartache. In those cases, I'm the one running. Make your mistakes, but learn from them. I'm not writing this from up on my throne living my happily ever after. I'm still out there looking for love, pursuing my dreams, and aiming for the best life has to offer.

PART II: Shaping Up

DE **34** FRIENDED

Chapter Four

STAGE I: DETOX

"I don't know why they call it heartbreak. It feels like every other part of my body is broken too."
~Missy Altijd

Break ups suck, simply put. Whether you've been dating for six months or six years, we are wired to form connections and attachments to people that affect us deeply. When things don't work out, we are left in a state of despair, ripping ourselves apart wondering what's wrong with us and how someone who we loved so much could no longer feel that love in return.

While physically, your heart cannot actually break, the pain that accompanies the conclusion of a significant relationship can be brutal and wearing on all of the body's vital organs. Your brain feels overwhelmed with thoughts and emotions as a movie montage of the last few months plays through your mind; the pause button pushed repeatedly as you try to figure at which pivotal moment things went wrong and what you should have done differently. Your chest swells and tightens, causing a shortness of breath, and your whole body aches with a heavy sadness. Tears flow so frequently you begin to feel dehydrated, the skin around your eyes swelling then subsiding into a pool of darkness in the shadows on your face. What you may not realize is that these reactions are actually quite common, and serve as the body's defense to its sudden state of loss.

When a person falls in love, the levels of dopamine and oxytocin—which are responsible for our feelings of happiness and trust—rise to higher than normal levels. We tend to become addicted to this chemical rush, in the same way a junkie becomes addicted to cocaine—it makes us feel great in the moment. (Side note: This is the same hormone released in women when we have sex, hence where the attachment tends to come in.) At the end of a relationship, our body experiences withdrawal from these chemicals, and we enter a state of mind similar to a person deprived of food, water, or drugs. Our brain, the body's key motivational system, ignites irrational and involuntary behavior that may include mania, obsession, fear, and anxiety. These chemical changes also cause physiological effects on the autonomic nervous system, such as heart rate, blood flow, blood pressure, and digestion. The feeling that your stomach is in knots is quite accurate. Cortisol, the body's stress hormone, spikes, incurring fatigue and illness due to a weakened immune system. Therefore, your "heartbreak" is not simply an expression; the ending of this loving relationship causes legitimate pain throughout the body.

The connection between the mind and body is incredibly powerful, and the way a body reacts physically during a break up is medically comparative to how it deals in the case of death. Both situations involve losing a loved one, but in the case of a relationship ending, that person's ghost is still alive, breathing, and potentially screwing his new client. Many people will enter a temporary state of depression, where their body is overcome by feelings of exhaustion, dread about the future, upset stomach, and loss of appetite. And so we begin involuntary detox.

The Heartbreak Detox

During this initial phase, the first thing to go, aside from your sanity, is typically your appetite. Food seems irrelevant when your stomach and intestines are knotted so tightly there is no way anything can pass through to the point of digestion. If you happen to be someone who tends to gain weight post-break up, eating your way through the sadness, then it's even more pertinent for you to follow the shape up stages listed in this book.

Let me start by saying I am in no way advocating starving yourself nor am I a supporter of anorexia or bulimia. However, I am a realist—sometimes you simply need to eat to live and not live to eat, and during a time of crisis, it's important to get just enough food in you to keep your systems functioning while allowing your body to begin the healing process in whatever way is comfortable. In a survey I conducted amongst 18-35 year old women who had recently gone through a break up, 93.6% admitted to losing weight post-break up, with results ranging up to twenty pounds or more. For 61.3% of those women, the weight loss occurred over a three to eight week period, indicating how common it is to lose a significant amount of weight during a relatively short period of time. This weight loss is temporary if not recovered from properly.

The first stage is pretty simple and focuses solely on the healing and cleansing aspect of the break up—the Detox. Basically, let it all out. Cry as much as you need to. Sleep excessively. Drink massive amounts of tea and soup, but be sparing with the French fries, cookies, and ice cream. Make sure you consume loads of water during this time to keep your body and skin hydrated.

I consulted with NJ-based nutritionist Rachel Albaum, RD, MSN, on the top ten "super foods" that she recommends specifically for your body post-break up. If you are not consuming your normal caloric intake, your body is being robbed of vital nutrients that will further harm your internal systems, making it that much harder to repair in the next phase.

Here's what she had to say: "When under any type of stressful situation, our body becomes inflamed, which causes us to act out by either having food cravings, breaking out, or gaining weight in our abdominal section. The most important thing to counteract this is by treating your body kindly with healthy and nutritious foods. You want to avoid foods that cause sugar spikes —as mentioned above, this is only a temporary solution and in fact can lead to more depression and feelings of lethargy as your sugar high plummets!"

Rachel came up with several foods that require minimal cooking and less grocery store trips.

BREAK UP SUPERFOOD SHOPPING LIST

☐Eggs

☐Beans

☐Greens

☐Sweet Potatoes

☐Salmon/Tuna

☐Almonds/Walnuts

☐Whole Grains

☐Berries

☐Yogurt

☐Apples

Shopping List Breakdown

Eggs: One of the highest quality protein sources you can have, not to mention affordable and easy to prepare. Don't always skip the yolk! Although it has some extra calories, fat, and cholesterol, it's chock full of nutrients including Vitamin D, which you are probably lacking if you haven't made it out of bed.

Beans: Beans, beans they're good for your heart... Seriously, though! Lentils, chickpeas, kidney beans, etc. Another quick "go-to food." They are cheap and full of protein, fiber, calcium, potassium, and iron.

Greens: Spinach, broccoli, kale... take your pick. The darker the better! This super food is packed with Vitamins A, C, K, folate, iron, and calcium. FYI: Buying frozen vegetables are completely okay and, in fact, healthier. Studies show frozen veggies maintain their nutrients better than fresh; plus, when you don't want to get out of bed and go food shopping every few days for fresh ones, it makes them much more convenient!

Sweet Potatoes: Packed with tons of nutrients and last a long time when refrigerated. They are full of Vitamin A and beta-carotene, low in the glycemic index, and help keep you fuller longer with the lower sugar spike and high fiber content.

Salmon/tuna: Canned or pouched in water is okay. These omega-rich foods have been shown to help with depression, not to mention they work wonders for your hair, skin, and nails... all things you've probably been neglecting. Omega 3 fatty acids are a natural anti-inflammatory food, perfect for when you and your body are under stress.

Almonds/walnuts: Loaded with fiber and monounsaturated fats (healthy fats), Vitamin E and magnesium. Tip: Magnesium is useful to help you get a better sleep. Additionally, walnuts are a good source of omega 3 fatty acids.

Whole grains: 100% whole grains, that is. This includes oatmeal, brown rice, and whole grain breads. What you hear is true... Stay away from white bread, bagels, donuts, etc. Simple sugar may be something initially your body craves after a break up. This is because of hormone fluctuations that occur when these foods are eaten. But remember when you were little and you would eat a lot of candy and run around on a crazy "sugar high"? What you may have forgotten was the crash that came immediately after. This same thing occurs in adulthood, too. As you probably discovered by now, that "happy" effect is only temporary. After you've consumed these "simple" sugars and the elation is over, you're going to feel even worse! You want to try to avoid the sugar high. Choosing whole grain foods full of fiber will help you to maintain your sugar levels and also provide extra nutrients to fuel your body.

Berries: Strong antioxidant and flavanoids to help boost your immune system and reduce inflammation. Again, you can definitely get them frozen—add them to you oatmeal or into your yogurt or use them as a snack. Just make sure to purchase the berries that don't have added sugar.

Yogurt: Make sure it's low fat and low sugar —stay away from the "fruit on the bottom." My personal favorite is Greek yogurt because, along with the calcium and probiotics, it is great source of protein. Probiotics are useful during a time of stress to rebuild the flora in your gut and pump up your immune system.

Apples: An apple a day keeps the doctor away and also keeps you from crunching on those chips. It is full of fiber and considered low in the glycemic index, which helps prevent you from having food cravings.

Above all, go easy on yourself. Talk to your friends and family, but also take some time for yourself to reflect. There will be days that you don't want to get out of bed. There will be moments when you don't want to eat. While you need to take care of your body to the best of your ability, you also need to let it go through its natural stages of grieving. One of the most frustrating things I encountered as I was trying to get over my relationship was everyone's "timeline." It seemed that every self-help book I frantically read and every person I turned to for advice expected me to magically turn off the part of my brain that was devastated by the ending of the relationship in a two week period of time. If I wasn't feeling better after a few weeks, I felt like a failure. So not only had I just failed at my relationship, I was also failing at my break up by not moving on quick enough.

Rule of Thumb: Do what your body tells you. People recover in their own way and time. Nobody knows YOU better than you. Always remember that.

In the meantime, move on to the next step....

Get HIM Out of Your Face Detox

Now comes the detoxing of your significant other. For this pain, I blame Mark Zuckerberg. Before the invention of Facebook, a break up was kept between two people and the family and friends they opted to tell in their own time. Now the ending of a relationship on Facebook leads to public humiliation in front of 500-1,000 of your closest friends and colleagues, followed by comments, "Likes," and the inevitable e-mail from your ex-boyfriend who is now notified that you are single. Since Jack never really "loved me" enough to actually want to be in a committed relationship, I never had to go through this humiliation. Instead, I had to face the embarrassment of all of my friends and family and for that matter, his friends and family, watching the harem of women fighting for his attention on his Facebook wall, all the while knowing how I felt about him. What a crock of shit. If you need a Facebook wall to prove to your relationship to the world, you are simply overcompensating for what you are lacking. It's like listening to guys talk about how big their penis is. If you have to point it out to people, it's probably because you are lame, insecure, and have a small dick. Therefore, my conclusion is the more times you post on your girlfriend's wall or she posts on yours, the smaller your penis is.

My advice would be to never post a relationship status until you are married, but if you have already done so, do yourself a favor and remove this privately. I have watched many friends lose their minds over the discovery that their ex took down his relationship status anywhere from the day after to three months after the initial break up. I've also heard of people learning that they were broken up with via Facebook status, which is just downright humiliating. If this has happened to you, give yourself an extra week of Detox, because you were dating a real asshole.

Next comes the removal of his contact info from your phone. Even if you have his number memorized, it still takes that much more effort to type it in during a moment of weakness and despair. One night I angrily texted an ex after a few cocktails, only to receive one back the next morning that I was texting the wrong person. Big thanks to the Universe for intervening on that embarrassing situation.

Now, another option to deleting the number (because, let's be honest, you're going to dial it whether it's deleted or not) is to change his name in your phone. During one of my beloved girls' nights, my friends begged me to replace one particular guy's number in my phone with one of theirs, so JUST IN CASE I was tempted to text him, it would default to them. I thought this might get tricky and a little confusing, so I came up with an alternative solution—I changed his name in my phone. And not to Paul or Chris, but to "Bad Idea." Here are some other options... Feel free to tailor it to your specific situation.

Cell Phone Alias' for Your Ex

Man Whore

Pathological Liar

Mind Fuck

Crazy Town

Heart Ache

NO

You get the picture.

So else how do you keep yourself mentally healthy during this critical period? Most likely, you don't. But you will eventually. That's what your friends, this book, and Stages II-IV are for.

It's tough, I know.

A few years back the book "He's Just Not That Into You" came out, and millions of heartbroken girls scrambled to finally get the answer to that plaguing question "WHY???" It was followed by the also successful cult-hit

"It's Called a Break Up Cause It's Broken," another Bible for the newly single. What's crazy is that those books are now somewhat dated, due in part to the incredible advances in technology and use of social networking. Facebook was merely a glimmer in the eye of Mark Zuckerberg (or the Winklevoss twins, depends which team you're on) and a tweet was simply the sound a bird makes early in the morning. Now those two sites, in addition to e-mail, texting, blogging, iChat, G-Chat, FB chat, Skyping, Pinterest, Google+, Spotify, YouTube, and everything else under the sun, have made it impossible to seamlessly slip away from your ex without some sort of glaring reminder. I remember staring angrily at the faded camera on my iChat Buddy List, wondering what girl he was video chatting with this time. We deleted and re-added each other from Facebook so many times as "friends" that upon my last, triumphant defriending of him and his new girlfriend, I got a personal message from Mark Zuckerberg that said:

Dear Christina,

You are officially cut off from re-adding Jack as a friend. Clearly, you are not friends. Let it go.

Love,
Mark

Defriending him on Facebook was just a minor piece of the puzzle, though. In my case, he was not just a part of my social network on the Internet, but he was also a huge part of my social network in real life. We would run into each other at least once a week out with mutual friends, and due to our careers and our completely dysfunctional relationship with no concept of boundaries, it was really difficult to act cool. That was a huge part of the reason my Detox only lasted briefly.

Which brings me to my next point: The Detox Stage is only temporary. Similar to the Blue Print Cleanse™ I tried in fall of 2009, Detox is only meant to happen once and then move on. It's what you do AFTER the Detox that makes the most lasting impact.

The Blue Print Cleanse™ is an all-juice detox that you can consume anywhere from one to seven days. You purchase pre-packaged bottles that are delivered to your door, and you must drink ONLY these six beverages/ meals/concoctions for the selected number of days. I chose three, and for those seventy-two hours I filled my body with water, green juice, and the occasional piece of gum. Ah, the things we do to our minds and bodies in the name of "health." After my jaunt with Blue Print Cleanse™, I was feeling so great I decided to adopt some new, permanent changes to my eating habits. I cut out meat all together, opting for a pescatarian diet (which is basically vegetarian, but I'll occasionally eat fish), stopped using sugar substitutes, and abstained from packaged candy (Skittles, Twizzlers, etc). It was hard, but for over a year, I did not touch so much as a gummy bear. Now and then I'll indulge sparingly, but I know my limits and if I think there's any chance I'll binge, I throw those suckers in the garbage and don't look back.

Think of your ex as a gummy bear. The longer you're able to go without him, the easier it will be to resist him when he's sitting on the shelf of Duane Reade, calling to you mercilessly during a serious case of PMS.

If You Don't Believe Me, Ask Them...

In a survey, I asked, "If you could go back in time, what's the one thing you would have done differently post-break up?" The following page lists the top ten responses.

Top 10 Break Up Mistakes

10. "Find a way to inspire yourself and take yourself out of the relationship you were just in, like a new hobby, or traveling. Breaking the codependency was the hardest part."

9. "Not have been so ruthlessly mean."

8. "Had more self-confidence to see it wasn't my fault and that I'd lost my sense of self."

7. "Broken up sooner."

6. "Got mad instead of sad and realized I'd dodged a bullet!"

5. "Try not to compare myself to the 'new woman.'"

4. "Not tried to get back together with him over and over again." (This was an overwhelmingly common answer.)

3. "I wouldn't have drunk texted/called/emailed him. Or slept with him. Idiot."

2. "Cut off all communication."

And my personal favorite—1. "Kill him."

Technology Talks

32% of women surveyed listed "stalking Facebook/Twitter" as the hardest habit to break post-break up. Other responses included:

- Sharing everything that happens with the person.
- Reaching for the phone to call—it's so hard not to do that.
- IMing/texting the person. Not only is it something you are used to doing, it's just so EASY to do it.
- Adjusting to sleeping alone.
- Not trusting someone new.
- Constantly being self-deprecating. It took me a long time to remember that I was fun, and worth being with and loving.

See? You're not alone.

Chapter Five

STAGE II: REPAIR

"Have you ever been hurt and the place tries to heal a bit, and you just pull the scar off of it over and over again?" ~Rosa Parks

For most of my dating history, I was the poster child for being the "rebound girl." Seriously. At one point I thought there might have been a mass e-mail circulating with my picture and the caption, "If you are damaged, emotionally unavailable, and on the rebound, please date me." Some were brief flings, others were more lengthy endeavors, but the outcome was always the same: they ran. Wil. E. Coyote/Road Runner dust cloud-style. Sometimes without notice. Always leaving me ripping myself apart, replaying everything I did wrong, analyzing every aspect of my existence until I finally deemed myself unworthy and incapable of being loved. One time a few years back, a friend of mine was going through a bad break up. His fiancée had just left him and within weeks I could sense his attraction to me. I resisted, knowing the timing was bad and it had more to do with his loneliness and self-pity and less to do with being in a relationship with me. I gave it almost a year, and when he was still showing interest I caved, figuring he'd had time to sow his oats. Wrong. We hooked up for a few months, just enough time for me to really start liking him, and then out of the blue he stopped returning my calls. A few weeks later, I ran into him with another woman. They are now married and have a baby. Rumor was she had a drinking problem and occasionally turned violent. The only thing that seemed to bother him about me was I had matching placemats at my old apartment. I still don't know why he stopped calling.

In the past, I turned to food for comfort in those times of depression. I figured, "Hey, no one wants to see me naked anyway, what difference does it make?" It makes a huge difference—if you don't have respect for yourself and your body, how can you expect someone else to have respect for those things?

The patterns we engage in that sabotage our weight loss efforts are quite similar to the patterns we engage in that sabotage a successful break up. Recognize the similarities between your relationships with food and your relationships with people, and it will become easier to decipher what went wrong and how to change your approach.

I have been dieting since I was twelve years old. I wish this was an exaggeration, but unfortunately it's a cold, hard fact. Weight Watchers, The Grapefruit Diet, Atkins, South Beach, The Zone, Fit For Life, lo-carb, no-carb, only carb, diet pills, laxatives, and juice cleanses galore. My dieting history reads like the "Who's Who of Eating Disorders Anonymous." As a dancer, shoving my body into pink tights and a fitted leotard day after day spurred an abundance of body image issues, and I was constantly on a quest to be "skinny." It became an addiction. After ballooning up in college to my highest weight, I was consumed with trying to drop those stubborn, beer and pizza-laden pounds. Nothing worked. It seemed the more I tried to make my food relationship work, the less successful I was. Sound familiar? Think for a moment about the people you've fallen for. My list consisted of the Athlete, the Old School Italian, the Construction Worker, the Intellect, the Artist... On paper, they all had promise. In person, they were like multiple wrecking balls to my heart. Yet, when each of those dating efforts failed, I blamed myself... just as I did with my diets. If those eating plans worked for other people, why didn't they work for me?

Time For Change

The key to shaping up physically lies in the Repair and Strengthen Stages. Emotionally, it may take you much longer to fully recover from a bad break, but in the meantime you can make your body slamming, your skin glow, your hair shine, and your ass tight enough to bounce a quarter off of it. Doesn't that sound nice? It does, doesn't it? I'm still trying to master that last one.

Now, be honest with yourself... I'm sure in those months or years of domestic love and bliss, you packed on a few pounds because you grew "comfortable." Why do we do that to ourselves? Losing your sense of self in a relationship can also come in a physical form. You feel able to let yourself go because you found love, and love knows no flaws. FALSE. First of all, love does know flaws. Men who are in relationships do not incur a sudden loss of sight. An ex once reminded me, "Men are visual people," as I scrambled to turn off the lights. One of our most powerful weapons as women is that our bodies are perceived as artwork to men. Even the gay ones. They want to touch and experience every ounce of you, gaze in pleasure, and show you off to their friends. Then the prick dumps you and you become a less attractive version of the cracked out homeless person sleeping on the subway in a pile of his own urine. Why give them that satisfaction?

Before you even begin to think about Repairing, you must shake it off and get yourself feeling fabulous again. Your body will come along in its own time, but for now, let's get you back to that pretty, smart, and happy person everyone knows and loves.

Repair Stage Checklist

☐Get a haircut, color, or both.
☐Mani/pedi with the girls. (Booze optional.)
☐Sign up for a class.
☐Plan a trip.
☐Volunteer.

---

1. *Get a haircut, color, or both.* If you don't want to change your style, just go for a trim, or have it washed and blown out before a big night out with the girls. Chances are you

haven't been doing a lot of showering lately, and it's incredible how a few snips of the scissors and some aptly placed products can break you out of even your deepest funk. Right after, make sure to snap a hot self-pic and Instagram the shit out of it so everyone can comment on how great you look.

2. *Manicure/pedicure.* Grab your girlfriends and make a date out of it. Bonus points if you can find a salon that serves booze and a massage to boot.

3. *Sign up for a class.* ANY class. I took lots of classes and picked up a number of new hobbies during every break up I went through, including photography, Italian (classes, not men), pole dancing, anti-gravity yoga, baking, football, kickboxing, Pilates, spin, surfing, running, and hip hop to name a few. In each activity, you should push yourself to your limit and give it your all. (I may be slightly competitive.) You'll be happy you did in the end, as you'll emerge stronger and more powerful than when you began... It's liberating and exciting all at once! Plus, it's a great way to meet new people and expand your social circle to include friends not associated with "He whose name we shall not mention."

4. *Plan a trip.* Whether it's a short weekend to the beach with your girlfriends or a solo trip to Italy, "Eat, Pray, Love" style, getting away for a brief period from everything that reminds you of your ex is not only healthy, but sometimes necessary.

5. *Volunteer.* Go to your local homeless shelter, plan a trip abroad, or take one afternoon a week to work with underprivileged children sharing your talents and expertise. If you are an athlete, look into coaching; if you're an artist, check out some after school programs that need mentors. Does your job consume most of your time? Pick an organization to donate to and raise money for that cause. Helping does heal, as cliché as it sounds. Seeing people who are struggling and living under far worse conditions than you changes the way you look at things. Sometimes you just need a little perspective.

Moving Along

Now that your mind and heart are in as good a place as they can possibly be, let's take a look at that body. The first step to maintaining the sudden weight loss you achieved during that first month of devastation is to find a balance. Balance is truly the key to all healthy living, and for that matter, all healthy relationships. Eat when you're hungry; stop when you're full. Indulge when you're craving something so you don't end up overeating later. Seems simple enough, right?

Wrong. One of the key reasons weight loss fails is because the creators of these plans put the fear of God in you that one piece of chocolate cake during the wrong phase at the wrong time of day with the wrong fork will ruin everything. What happens is the dieter will fall off the wagon briefly, and discouraged by failure, continue down the path of self-destruction. Newsflash: It's not the dessert you allow yourself on your birthday or the extra serving of whipped cream once a month on your hot cocoa that's preventing you from getting into your skinny jeans. Most likely, it's the nibbles, bites, tastes, and slivers that you sneak in between those special occasions that are causing beads of sweat to form as you frantically tug your jeans over your widened thighs, finally collapsing in a pile of tears sobbing, "What did I do wrong? I hate my life!"

Relationship Parallel: It's not the act of breaking up with your ex that has made it impossible for you to move on. It's the texting/stalking/obsessing/sleeping with them one last time. Defriend. And keep your clothes on.

Everything in Moderation

Saint Augustine said, "Complete abstinence is easier than perfect moderation." Abstinence requires picking one decision and sticking to it, while moderation means making choices. Typically when choosing between the angel and the devil of your stomach and your heart, the devil always wins... We always seem to want what's bad for us. So the goal of the Repair Stage? Moderation. That is the absolute best way to lose and maintain. Look at most of the women walking around Europe. There's a reason why their size two is cut significantly smaller than the Gap's size two, and that is because European women are naturally thinner. They walk everywhere, they eat smaller portions, they indulge in what they want and they don't look back. They simply live their lives, and food is just another part of it.

As I mentioned in the first chapter, the first few months after Jack broke up with me I did not approach the weight loss in a healthy way. After the Christmas Eve dumping and the revealing of a certain new girl repeatedly blowing up his Facebook wall, friending our mutual friends, and tagging pictures of the two of them together, I quickly spiraled downhill. He denied they were anything more than friends, saying she was just "light and fun," apparently two things I was not. The pictures of her and various other girls continued to appear and I would repeatedly feel more and more nauseous; eventually losing count of the number of times I threw away full meals or didn't even bother cooking because I was so disgusted. Yet, I kept going back. Because everyone told me it was just a "phase," and I was certain if I played my cards right, lost more weight, and looked super hot he would eventually realize what he had lost and would come running back. He ran, all right, into the arms of numerous women.

For those first six months, I adopted a steady diet of Strawberry Frosted Mini Wheats and hummus with pita chips. No joke. Maybe the occasional string cheese and piece of fruit thrown into the mix. On top of being an emotional wreck, I was running a stressful business and working two other jobs, so keeping busy was not an issue. However, as a business owner I had an unfortunate amount of time on my own to think, dwell, and stalk the Internet. While I was the thinnest I'd been in years, I'm pretty sure my vital organs were about to go on strike from malnutrition.

Although a twisted part of me reveled in the fact that my bones were sticking out of my chest, I also had to acknowledge that I wasn't healthy and that something had to change.

Eat to Live

Changing your eating habits post-break up is also a major component of shaping up. Most of these tips come from common sense, trial and error, and just understanding basics of how the body reacts during "crisis" mode. There are six key facts that you must stick to in order to make a noticeable difference in your newfound lifestyle.

Repair Rules

☐ **Variety is key.**
☐ **Eat to live, don't live to eat.**
☐ **Toss your "fat" clothes.**
☐ **Get moving.**
☐ **Stop when you're full.**
☐ **Throw it out.**
☐ **Fat is your friend. (In moderation)**

1. *Variety is key.* Boredom leads to "cheating," much like in a relationship. Your body is your new boyfriend… Keep it happy.

2. *Eat to live, don't live to eat.* Quite simply, the less you THINK about food, the less you will consume. I know that sounds very New Age and plant-worshipper, "think yourself thin," but it's true. I kept the weight off because I stopped obsessing over what I was eating every second of the day. I threw out my food diary, stopped reading every label, and

rarely got on a scale. If my pants felt tight, I cut back a little. If I wanted a cookie, I ate one. I stopped letting FOOD control my life and instead, I controlled my life.

3. *Toss your "fat" clothes.* Once they are out of the closet, it's motivation to stay at your current weight. Who has the time and money to buy a new wardrobe every six months? The economy is in a crisis. Do your part and donate those baggy sweaters to someone in need and keep your savings account in check by staying one size.

4. *Get moving.* I'll address this more in the next stage, Strengthen, but exercise is a huge factor in healthy bodies, if not the most important. Not only is it good for your heart, muscles, and general well being, it can also serve as a wonderful stress reliever and regular distraction from your pain.

5. *Stop when you're full.* "Seriously?" you're thinking right now. "What kind of lame advice is that? Of course I stop when I'm full." No, you don't. You eat mindlessly until someone finally clears your plate or you are forced to walk away from the table. Portion sizes in America are out of control. You need to become much more aware of your body in order for this to be successful, but it can happen. Not to mention, you will realize

how much better you feel when you walk away from the table and don't feel coma-induced or the need to throw up.

6. *Throw it out.* I don't care that there are children starving in Ethiopia. If you think it's going to tempt you, get rid of it. I'm sure my ancestors would be livid to see the beautiful meals and desserts that have gone straight to the dumpster after just a few bites. But I know myself and my level of willpower and sometimes it just needs to not be there. Sort of like my ex.

7. *Fat is your friend.* For years I lived off fat-free, chemically-enhanced food products. Butter spray on toast? Yes please. Fat-free cheese that's a by-product of the plastic family? Yum. Melt that shit all over my Egg Beaters and Weight Watchers bread that's only one point. Candy craving? Grab a bag of sugar-free jelly beans chock full of cancer-causing agents and not digestible by any natural enzymes. Also, grab a container of TUMS.

Do yourself a favor. Never buy that shit again. It's like sleeping with your creepy neighbor just to have a warm body in the bed, when you really want the beautiful man who frequents your local coffee shop and you've never had the balls to talk to. Go for the real thing, always. In food, in dating, in life. Isn't it better to have one great date with a guy you really dig, then a bunch of meaningless nights with a guy that makes your uterus shudder in disgust? Same with food- you'll be more satisfied with a bite of that made-from-scratch chocolate cake than any amount of fat-free, sugar-free, preservative-filled, plastic-wrapped Little Debbie snack pack.

Reality Check

When I moved to NYC, I was both horrified by and grateful for the calorie labels in all of the restaurants. It made me realize that I was consuming WAY more than I should be for my height and weight, and definitely encouraged me to make different choices. It's also a VERY expensive city, so I was forced to only eat when I was hungry if I wanted to make rent. Not that this is going to be the case for you. Each person has different patterns, habits, restrictions, and general lifestyles. A reason why so many "diet plans" don't work is that they don't address the general population. Whether you're a stay-at-home mom or a workaholic lawyer, you most likely don't have the time to sit and plan out every meal and every morsel that grazes your lips. The key is to train yourself into making good choices WITHOUT thinking, that way it becomes habit. For me, things changed for the better when I finally moved into my own apartment with a kitchen, a luxury I was without for close to three years. Food shopping once a week and pre-cooking certain parts of the meal saved me time and money, and made food and eating less of a focus in my day.

Think about the first few months after you broke up with the love of your life. You hated sleeping in that bed alone, didn't you? It was in those dark, late night moments that you were probably most tempted to call your ex, just to see what he was up to/find out if he was miserable and sleeping alone too. Eventually, you got used to it. In fact, you discovered it was quite nice to be able to sprawl out, and not be awoken in the middle of the night by his incessant snoring and selfish hogging of the covers. The addiction waned.

Same goes for food. Most of the things we struggle to cut out, we fight with because they are habits, not necessarily things we enjoy. I didn't enjoy getting my heart broken over and over again any more than I enjoyed gaining and losing the same fifteen pounds for the past ten years. But on some level, that weight was as comfortable as that relationship, and it took a huge leap of faith to trust I would be happier without both.

Table For One, Please

One of the things that can lead to weight GAIN after a break up is that you may now be dining alone. Though it's fairly simple to make a portion-sized meal for one, it's often easier to just order take out. Some people also eat more when they are not under the watchful eye of others (we call them closet eaters), and being single makes it very easy to stop paying attention to what you're shoveling in your mouth. Last I checked, the spare pillows don't really care if you're bloated when you wrap your arms around them at night. A few tips to keep this under control, please?

1. *Drink more water.* For one, it's great for your skin and digestive system. Also, it's the lowest calorie option out there, and who wants to waste their daily caloric intake on Pepsi? There was a powerful ad campaign a few years back on the NYC subway. It demonstrated how much sugar is in your favorite soft drinks by displaying a lemon-flavored soft drink pouring out and turning into layers of gooey fat as it hits the glass. Yeah. That gave me nightmares for months. Effective, though.

Go for coffee, tea, unsweetened iced tea, or flavored water (throw in one of those great new packets by Crystal Light or Benefiber for added health benefits!) when getting your hydration on.

2. *Dine out with friends, or invite them over for a home-cooked meal.* It will keep your mind and hands busy living in the present, instead of mindlessly munching and obsessing over your tool of an ex. Dinner parties are always fun, and they're also great ways to pass the time when you're feeling a bit lonely. An entire day can be spent shopping, prepping, cooking, eating, drinking wine and then cleaning up. Next thing you know, twenty-four hours have passed and you haven't looked at your ex's Twitter feed once.

3. *Take a walk after a meal, whether it be breakfast, lunch or dinner.* There are so many health benefits to this I can't even begin. You add cardio to your day, get fresh air, clear your mind and allow for a moment of Zen with the Universe, aid digestion, burn calories, and tone your body all in one shot. Walking after a meal is a great form of therapy. So plan out your next route and get to it.

I'll Take That To Go

If you're a working girl, the majority of your meals are probably eaten on the go. Now that you aren't meeting your boyfriend, aka the Human Garbage Pail, for lunch breaks, you have a much wider selection of where to go and what to choose. I picked out my favorite on-the-go meals for the girl who can't stop moving... All are waistline and wallet friendly.

** Fun Fast Food Fact: If you are absolutely dying for fast food, get a kids meal. Smaller portion size means less calories and fat, but you'll still curb the craving for that greasy, fatty food without doing too much damage to your stomach and your psyche. **

**Healthy Alternatives That Won't Break
The Bank or the Belly**

☐ *Jamba Juice*- Acai Super Antioxidant, 16 oz.: 260 calories.
☐ *Starbucks*- Tall Nonfat Latte: 90 calories, Spinach, Roasted Tomato, Feta, and Egg White Wrap: 280 calories
☐ *Qdoba Mexican Grill*- Grilled Veggie Burrito, Naked, with black beans, cheese, and pico de gallo: 380 calories
☐ *Dunkin Donuts*- Medium Coffee with Skim Milk and Splenda: 30 calories, Multigrain Bagel: 390 calories, with reduced fat cream cheese.
☐ *Whole Foods Sushi*- Avocado cucumber roll: 158 calories, Brown rice California roll: 177 calories, Brown rice Spicy Tuna Avocado roll: 189 calories, Rainbow roll: 186 calories, Spicy Shrimp Tempura roll: 193 calories, Edamame: 50 calories.
☐ *Panera Bread*- You Pick Two- Low-Fat Vegetarian Black Bean Soup: 170 calories, Half Asian Sesame Chicken Salad: 200 calories.
☐ *Au Bon Pain*- Turkey and Swiss on a Farmhouse Roll (Half Sandwich): 320 calories, Medium Diet Pepsi: 0 calories, Small Fruit Cup: 70 calories.

I'm In Repair...

Oh, John Mayer. You sure do know how to write a break up song. The concept of the Repair stage is to take the proper steps to fix your body both inside and out. Your mind and your heart will always be the last thing to heal, and you need to approach your break up, weight loss, and fitness routine with that in mind. The most important thing to remember is to give yourself time. Go easy. Don't beat yourself up if you have a rough night and consume an entire pint of Ben & Jerry's Chocolate Chip Cookie Dough Ice Cream. It happens. Tomorrow, cut back a little. Skip the mid-afternoon latte and just have a plain cup of tea. Your body will quickly bounce back from the minor damage that pint brought on.

...I'm Not Together, But I'm Getting There

Congratulations! You may not feel it, but you've actually taken HUGE strides in becoming a stronger, healthier, and more powerful YOU. It's hard to feel that way post-break up—when you're scrutinizing every detail and action of what went down those last few months, but trust me when I say the most important mantra to adopt is "Success is the best revenge." Take control of your life, and your food habits and relationship habits will no longer control you.

Now that your insides are full of healthy quantities of food and nutrients, your skin is radiating post-facial, and your hair is shining and strong, let's get your body tight, toned, and ready for action.

Real Women Weigh In

I asked the following question in a survey to a random group of women: "During periods of great sadness and depression, what kinds of foods do you find yourself craving?"

- 34.2% - Sweets: Cookies, Ice Cream, Cake, Chocolate, etc.
- 21.1% - Salty: Chips, Pretzels, Cheese, etc.
- 21.1% - Comfort: Meat and potatoes, mac and cheese, pizza, etc.
- 21.1% - Booze
- And the largest response: 39.5% - I usually lose my appetite completely.

Diet Fact:

The top three things women list as the hardest part about trying to lose weight are:

- Portion Sizes.
- Cutting Down on the Booze.
- Constantly Thinking About What You're Eating.

Chapter Six

Stage III: STRENGTHEN

"Oh, my friend, it's not what they take away from you that counts. It's what you do with what you have left." ~Hubert Humphrey

So you're officially a "dumpee." This does not give you an excuse to be "dumpy." If nothing else motivates you to get yourself back to working out and eating well, try this on for size: You're going to have to be naked in front of someone new eventually. And he may want to keep the lights on.

Despite being a dancer and certified Pilates trainer, I truly loathe going to the gym. Unless I'm taking a class, it's incredibly boring to me. Who wants to throw themselves on a machine for an hour, walking, running, biking, and climbing furiously only to stay in one spot the whole time? Lame.

This stage is all about the action. I've devised a number of workout ideas, App suggestions, playlists, and exercise alternatives that will motivate even the laziest person to suck it up and break a sweat. Every option is designed to keep your mind and body engaged at all times, helping you to forget about your ex for the time being and focus on toning, sculpting, and releasing those beautiful endorphins that leave us high on life. There is a smattering of do-it-yourself at home workouts, ideas for the gym, and of course, my favorite classes of all time (most can be found in a city near you). The best part about it? You get to design it. Let's face it; sometimes it's hard to follow a routine perfectly. Everyone's body is shaped differently and what's comfortable and works for Sue may not work for Cathy. It's up to you to pick and choose which ones work best for you. Perk: It keeps your mind stimulated and give you something new to talk about next time you're having brunch with your friends, because let's be honest... they're probably sick of talking about your ex. Plus, it allows you to maintain a variety so you can conceivably do a different workout every day. Studies have shown we are more likely to stick with something if we don't get bored. Think of this as an exercise buffet!

But I Don't Have The Time...

Stop it. Yes you do. Do you have time to sit for an hour obsessively stalking his Facebook page looking for evidence of a new girlfriend? Then yes, you have the time to work out. At least stand at the computer and do some squats while you are destroying your sanity and self-worth. Guys like a little crazy as long as they have a nice ass. Need a little motivation? Here's a list of ideas for all fitness types to get their butt in gear, collected from years of weight loss groups, Google research, dance teachers, trainers, and of course, personal experience.

Strengthen Stage Starters

☐Lay it out the night before.
☐Take advantage of your lunch break.
☐Plan it around your favorite TV show.

---

1. If you are a morning person, lay out your sneakers and workout clothes before you go to bed at night. Place them in a spot where you would actually trip over them to get to the bathroom. Then, after you trip, put them on. And get moving.

2. For those that work in the corporate world, take advantage of your lunch break. A lot of Pilates and Yoga studios offer lunchtime classes, a great option if you don't want to end up a drenched, sweaty mess but still want to target all of those hard to reach muscles. Short on cash? Take a few months and do free trials of new and trendy fitness studios that you can't afford. I used to work at one of those and honestly, it's brilliant. You keep variety in your routine, meet new people, get a good workout, and won't break the bank. I don't consider this a scam; I consider it an efficient and affordable way to not get royally ass-f%#d while trying to stay in shape living in an expensive city or town. You can also check online at sites like Living Social, Gilt City or Groupon for monthly specials at different fitness facilities in your city. Another idea: Pair up with a friend or acquaintance that's training for their Pilates/Yoga/group fitness certification. When I was getting certified, I was always looking for guinea pigs to torture and fill my required hours. Free for you, necessary for them. Win all around.

3. More of a night owl? Plan your workout around your favorite TV show. Whether you hop on the treadmill or do jumping jacks in your living room, you'll be shocked with how quickly the time goes when you are

distracted by an episode of "Girls." Bonus points if you work out during a sitcom—laughter burns calories! (Okay, that last part was a little cheesy, but it IS true.) (I love Friends.)

Your Very Own Exercise Buffet

Set the timer on your watch or cell phone for a half hour. Even better, create a playlist that lasts a half hour or longer. I've developed a few, but my taste in music may be wildly different from yours. It takes about five minutes to drag and drop your favorite songs into a playlist on iTunes, and you'll be surprised at how quickly your workout will go with the right soundtrack behind it.

Here is a small smidgeon of exercises that you can add to your routine. I also love ripping out the different 10/15/20 minute workouts they always feature in your favorite health magazines, like SELF, Fitness, Women's Health and SHAPE. Start a collection in a folder or for those more technologically savvy, bookmark them on your iPad. That way, you can refer back to them at a later date. If any of these exercises are unfamiliar to you, you can easily find them on YouTube to get a visual tutorial. I've also created an "on-the-go" fitness plan for the freelance exerciser, which you can find on my YouTube channel at www.youtube.com/ nycartscene. Look for the playlist, "Fall Fitness Fridays."

Savvy Strengthening-Mix and Match!

Ab-tastic
- ☐ The Hundred
- ☐ The Plank
- ☐ The Scissor
- ☐ The Reverse Curl

"Armed" and Dangerous
- ☐ 7/7/7
- ☐ Tricep Dips
- ☐ Push Ups
- ☐ Sculpted Shoulders

Bootylicious
- ☐ Ballerina Squat
- ☐ Standard Squat
- ☐ Can Can
- ☐ Butt Lift

Break a Sweat
- ☐ Workout DVD's/OnDemand
- ☐ Child's Play
- ☐ Hit the Pavement
- ☐ No More Couch Potato
- ☐ Killer Classes

Savvy Strengthening Break Down

AB-tastic

The Hundred: A traditional Pilates move, the hundred targets those deep abdominal muscles and can be modified for any level. Begin lying on your back with your legs in a tabletop position, knees bent. If you would like more of a challenge, straighten your legs and lower them to a 45-degree angle. Do not press your lower back into the floor, instead maintain a natural curve and think about pulling your belly button into your spine. Curl up so your head and shoulders come slightly off the ground and extend your arms straight along your sides. Inhale for five and exhale for five as you pump your arms in a steady up and down motion. Do ten sets of ten, and you will feel the burn!

The Plank: Take a standard push up position with your hands about chest width apart and your feet extended straight behind your hips. Now hold this for anywhere from thirty seconds to a minute. While maintaining the position, pull your abdominals up to your belly button and keep your weight centered over your arms. This is one of the best full body toning exercises out there. As you become more advanced you can add leg lifts and knees pulls to the standard plank.

The Scissor: Great for the obliques! Lie on your back with your hands placed behind your head. Bring your knees in toward the chest. As you extend your left leg, straight lift and twist your left elbow to meet the right knee. Now switch. Do this for three sets of twenty reps on each side.

The Reverse Curl: Lying on your back with your legs straight up at a 90-degree angle, place your hands flat by your side. Slowly lower your legs, controlling your abdominals and not letting your back arch up off the floor. When you feel you've reached your lowest point of control, slowly bring them back up. Do two sets of twenty to tone that hard-to-flatten lower belly.

"Armed" and Dangerous

7, 7, 7: Take two 5-10 lb weights or a 10-12 lb body bar. Holding the weight in both hands with your palms facing forward, curl your arms from a straight position just to the waist and then lower. Repeat seven times. Now hold the weights at the waistline, and only curl from the waist up to the chest. Repeat seven times. Now take the full range of motion bicep curl from the thighs to the chest. Repeat seven times. Do the whole thing twice through.

Tricep dips: Find a chair or bench. Place both hands with fingertips forward on the chair and walk yourself out so you are in a seated position in the air. Your feet can be flat or you can rest on your heels for added resistance. Bending at the elbows, drop down and press back up, not letting your body do any of the work—just your arms. Repeat fifteen times.

Good Ole Push Up: An oldie but goodie. Hands should be no wider than chest width apart, head in line with the spine, abdominals pulled in, and weight over the arms. Lower down and press back up, exhaling as you go. Your legs can be straight behind or you can modify the push up by resting on your knees. Make sure to keep your weight forward and your back nice and straight, not dropping your head. Two sets of fifteen reps to start. You can always add more as you get stronger.

Sculpted Shoulders: Take two 5-8 lb weights and place one in each hand. Bring your arms up to make a T shape, then bend at the elbows to bring your hands in line with your head, forming a goal post shape. Lift both weights up to meet directly over the crown of your head and then lower to the starting goal post position. Repeat for two sets of ten to fifteen reps.

Bootylicious

Ballerina Squat: Stand with your legs rotated out to your comfort level, your feet a little wider than your hips. Take a practice squat to make sure the knees are lined up right over the toes and not rolling in. Do two sets of fifty squats to tone inner and outer thighs as well as your butt. Add a 15-20 lb hand weight for resistance.

Standard Squat: With feet and knees lined up in a parallel position and hip width apart, bend at the knees and lean slightly forward until you feel the muscles in your butt activate. Return to your starting position. You can add three to five pound hand weights for added resistance. Two sets of fifteen reps is a good starting point.

Can Can: Lying on your side with your legs straight, bring your feet so they are slightly diagonal in front of your hips. Your hips should be perfectly stacked, one on top of the other. Prop up onto your side using your elbow, or lay flat and rest your head on your outstretched arm. Now bend the bottom leg in toward you and lift the top leg up, slightly bent. Take the heel of the top leg and drop it to the floor in front of your resting leg, working only from the knee. Now lift it up and repeat. The only part of your body that should be moving is from the knee down to the ankle. Do two sets of ten reps and then switch to the other side.

Butt Lift: Get down on all fours, with your knees directly under your hips and your wrists directly under your shoulders. Take your right leg off the ground, keeping the knee bent and facing the floor, and press the heel flat toward the ceiling. Now lift and lower your leg, keeping your heel flat and the knee bent, as though you are pressing your heel to the sky. Do this ten times slowly and then take ten small pulses. Repeat. Switch sides and do two sets on the left.

Break a Sweat

The cardio plan needs to be something fun and something that will hold your interest, which is going to differ from person to person. I would aim for at least twenty to thirty minutes of cardio with any of your freelance workouts. If running on a wheel like a gerbil doesn't appeal to you, check out any of these options.

Workout DVDS or Exercise TV On Demand: There are hundreds of videos out there with workouts that range in difficulty, time, and activity. Pick a few and alternate them. The more variety you put into your routine, the more muscles you will target and the quicker you will see results. You don't need a lot of space, either. My first apartment in NYC was a 13' x 9' studio furnished with a bed, table, desk, bookshelf, dresser, and chairs. I still managed to get my workouts in, though I guess it's a good thing I had already lost some weight at that point. Plus, when you're by yourself in your house or apartment, you can look as ridiculous and uncoordinated as you want. I have often laughed at myself imagining what people would think if they could see me walking in place or practicing hip hop moves in my living room for forty-five minutes. I also laughed when I started buying smaller sizes. It's a good trade off.

Child's Play: Go to Target and invest in a jump rope, medicine ball, resistance bands, and light hand weights. Now go home and create your own little Road Rules challenge. Making it up as you go is half the fun, and as long as you keep moving and using different props, you will be amazed with how quickly a normally boring workout can turn into a "Shape Up Extravaganza."

Hit The Pavement… Hard: I absolutely love exercising outdoors, and will do so in any weather condition. Rain or shine, I'll go for a walk or run. I also love to hike, bike ride, and would be up to learn tennis in the spring. Think of each step outside as a new adventure. It's a great way to improve your health and body while clearing your mind. Take a different route each time you head out in an effort to be inspired by something new. Lose track of time. The absolute best form of cardio, no matter what shape you are in or coordination level you have, is walking. So start there. Or if it's hard to get motivated, join a running group. You'll meet new people, learn new techniques, and have a set time to devote to working out each week.

No More Couch Potato: Don't want to miss your favorite primetime or morning shows? Here's a compromise, and a workout I adapted for the months when I was working from home in the dead of winter, living at my parents' place, with no gym membership. (Yes, those were good times.) Pick a 30-minute or an hour-long program. Hop on your elliptical/treadmill/bike or grab your sneakers and your jump rope. For every minute the show is on, do some form of cardio. I don't care if you have to run in place for 8 minutes, just keep moving. Jumping jacks, jump rope, mountain climbers, walking in place, dancing the twist.... No one can see you, so feel free to look as silly as need be. When the commercial comes on, stop your cardio and start toning. Pick any of the abs/butt/arm exercises listed or create your own. When the show comes back on, hop back to your cardio or pick a new activity. You will be amazed at how quickly the workout goes when you are stimulating your brain and body in every way.

Killer Classes: My other favorite thing to do is take a class, probably because of the dancer in me. I love the challenge of learning choreography or succeeding at something that didn't come easy at first. I've listed some of my favorite exercise classes I took over the course of my break up. Check your local gym and fitness clubs to see if they have a drop in or pay-per-class option, or ask a friend if you can come on their guest pass. A couple of years ago, a friend brought me to her Anti-Gravity Yoga class at Crunch Fitness. It was one of the hardest workouts I had ever done, but I felt like Pink at the 2011 Grammys when I mastered some of those moves. Pretty empowering.

Be a "Class Act"

☐ Anti-Gravity Yoga

☐ Boot Camp

☐ Pole Dancing

☐ Pilates

☐ Bikram Yoga

☐ Hip Hop

☐ Spinning

☐ Self-Defense

☐ Ballet

☐ Meditation

☐ Boot Camp

☐ Kickboxing

☐ Running groups

☐ Real Boxing

Ladies Choice

My survey showed the top five choices for favorite type of workout were as follows:

- Dancing
- Pilates/Yoga
- Running
- Cardio (machines)
- Aerobic classes

Get going today!

There's an App for That.

With the majority of people walking around with smart phones and tablets these days (you may be reading this book on one now), a great way to keep track of your shape up plan is with one of these great Apps. Some will also provide you with additional workout ideas, and most are free!

- Nike+ GPS
- iMap My Run
- Runkeeper
- Pocket Yoga
- Fitmodo
- Lose It!
- My Fitness Pal
- My Plate
- Workout Buddy

Music Makes the World Go Round.

Remember that Valentine's Day when you were sitting alone doing work at a local coffee shop, and the guy who broke your heart and the girl he was currently fucking walked passed and saw you through the window? And then after they spotted you, they came in to invite you to lunch with them? No? Just me? Well anyway, for those times when you just want to crawl into a dark abyss and cry until you forget your existence... There's a playlist for that.

Thanks to iTunes, making a playlist takes just seconds and can be catered to any type of mood or workout. I've compiled a few options as suggestions, and highly suggest you check out any artists you may not know to add to your collection. One playlist is our reader's choice from survey participants, another is dedicated to motivation and empowerment, and the third is designed for a hot bath, some candles, and lots of tissues.

READERS CHOICE
Playlist: *Ultimate Break Up*

- Toni Braxton, "Breathe Again"
- Natasha Bedingfield, "Happy"
- John Mayer, "Slow Dancing In a Burning Room"
- Tony Rich Project, "Nobody Knows"
- Rachel Yamagata, "Reasons Why"
- Rascal Flatts, "What Hurts The Most"
- Joanna Newsom, "On a Good Day"
- Evanescence, "Everybody's Fool"
- Lifehouse, "Broken"
- Donna Summer, "I Will Survive"
- Cee Lo, "Fuck You"
- Three Days Grace, "I Hate Everything About You"
- Sara Bareilles, "Basket Case"
- Coldplay, "The Hardest Part"
- OAR, "Shattered"
- Pearl Jam, "Come Back"
- Christina Aguilera, "Fighter"
- Carrie Underwood, "Before He Cheats"
- Sugarland, "Settlin"
- Jewel, "Please Don't Say I Love You"

CHRISTINA'S CHOICE
Playlist: *You Just Need a Good Cry*

- Bonnie Raitt, "I Can't Make You Love Me"
- James Morrison, "The Pieces Don't Fit Anymore"
- The Civil Wars, "Poison and Wine"
- Barnaby Bright, "Made Up Of"
- Tracy Chapman, "Smoke and Ashes"
- Missy Higgins, "Where I Stood"
- Annie Lennox, "Waiting In Vain
- Randy Newman, "Feels Like Home"
- Anna Krantz, "Rubble and the Dust"
- Patty Griffin, "Let Him Fly"
- David Gray, "Say Hello, Wave Goodbye"
- Carole King, "Will You Still Love Me Tomorrow"
- Martin Rivas, "Get Yourself Together"
- Amos Lee, "Learned A Lot"
- Adele, "Someone Like You"
- Bill Withers, "Ain't No Sunshine"
- Brandi Carlile, "That Wasn't Me"
- Madi Diaz, "A Little Bit"
- Jeff Buckley, "Lover, You Should Have Come Over"
- Fleetwood Mac, "Landslide"

CHRISTINA'S CHOICE
Playlist: *Motivation*

- Alanis Morissette, "You Oughta Know"
- Fun., "Some Nights"
- Adele, "Rumour Has It"
- Aerosmith, "Cryin' "
- Will Hoge, "Better Off Now (That You're Gone)"
- James Morrison, "Nothing Ever Hurt Like You"
- Kelly Clarkson, "Since You've Been Gone"
- Daughtry, "Over You"
- One Republic, "Good Life"
- Taylor Swift, "We Are Never Getting Back Together"
- Sara Bareilles, "Let the Rain"
- The Lumineers, "Classy Girls"
- Florence and the Machine, "Dog Days Are Over"
- Eminem, "Love the Way You Lie"
- Natasha Bedingfield, "Unwritten"
- Justin Timberlake, "Cry Me a River"
- Dixie Chicks, "Not Ready To Make Nice"
- Destiny's Child, "Survivor"
- Pink, "Blow Me (One Last Kiss)"
- Katy Perry, "Wide Awake"
- U2, "Still Haven't Found What I'm Looking For"

Chapter Seven

Stage IV: MAINTAIN

"Insanity is doing the same thing over and over again and expecting different results." ~*Albert Einstein*

If there were a pop culture awards show with a prize for the "Most Drawn Out Break Up," I would have been the winner for three consecutive years, hands down.

The number one reason break ups fail is because people go back to their exes in the heat of the moment or try to be "friends" before they are ready.

Rule of thumb: If he's seen you naked, he's not your friend.

And yes, break ups CAN fail. Take it from me.

Technically, I only dated Jack for a little under a year and we "broke up" consistently every few months for the next two and a half years that followed. By "break up," I mean we tried to stop sleeping together for the next two and a half years as my self-respect dwindled and his "friends with benefits" list grew. As my brother once pointed out, my break up lasted longer than most people's relationships do. Including my own.

The ending of our technical relationship began in December of 2007 and officially stopped in the summer of 2010. It took three states, multiple careers, being dropped for countless girls, and a six-week trip to Costa Rica to allegedly get him out of my system, and I STILL tried to be friends with him even when I returned. I was so high on myself for taking the time away to "heal" and be the bigger person that I approached him with a confidence and positive attitude that I was sure would be embraced wholeheartedly. For two years, he beat into my head that he JUST wanted to be friends, and couldn't understand why I had such issues with that. So I came home from the first of several trips to escape his presence and "find myself" and offered him the exact relationship he claimed he wanted, at which point he informed me he couldn't handle being friends with me and he preferred that I didn't contact him anymore... Despite the fact that we had a three and a half year history, all the same friends, worked in the same industry and saw each other, on average, twice a week. Yeah, that was going to work. In fact, my attempt to fix things between us and start fresh ended up starting another battle, for when I expressed this desire, he informed me that while I was gone he realized how much better his life was, that he finally felt free, and that he was miserable for the three years leading up to that point, which he blamed on me. Here I was, thinking I had been the person to save him from HIS horrible break up and flailing career, and his epiphany was that I was the cause for it. I can tell you honestly that those words hurt more than any amount of rejection I had ever encountered in my life. To have someone tell you that you are the reason for their unhappiness is an unfair and — to be quite frank — untrue burden to carry. As a wonderful friend of mine once pointed out, "Christina, you're amazing, but you do not have that kind of superhuman power over anyone. If he's miserable, it's his own fault."

I am still incredibly angry with him for dumping that on me, even after all these years. It felt like all those memories, good times, and special moments were just ripped away from me in a swift flash of light, my entire being trashed and the memory of me being "Eternal Sunshined" from his brain. He had erased me, and I had no say in it. I wanted to be the bigger person and support that he had found happiness. But when I became the scapegoat for his struggle, I hit my limit.

It turned out his cold, harsh severing of ties was a blessing. I lied to myself for a very long time because I thought that it made me strong to be his friend. It didn't. In fact, it made me psychotic. Because let's be honest here: Sex isn't just sex when you have loved or are still IN love with that person. No matter how hard you try to be the "cool" girl who can hook up with no strings attached, it NEVER works. Especially when less than twenty-four hours after what you perceived was this intense emotional connection, he shows up at your local bar with a girl he's actually interested in dating. And she isn't you.

Finally, I had to accept that all of those girls weren't just "phases." It didn't matter whether he loved them or not. What mattered was that he never really loved me. Because if he did, we would have been together. He would have wanted to make it work instead of running away each time we got close. Had I been a stronger, more secure person, I would have accepted this fact and moved on.

Even more so than love (or lack thereof), was that he also didn't respect me. Not in the relationship sense. And what I wanted even more than that love was for him to see the good, loyal and honest person I had always been toward him. I mean, fuck. I was tired of giving and giving and being the girl that no one wanted to be with. We both made a lot of mistakes along the way, mine usually appearing in the form of angry chimney text messages and embarrassing public outbursts upon seeing him with another woman. But when I finally realized how little he valued all the things that I DID value... it felt really shitty. Never shitty enough for me to fully walk away, though.

The real problem arises not when he starts loving someone else, but when you stop loving yourself.

One night at a dinner, I was sharing his revelations with a friend of mine who has been somewhat of a mentor and lived through a similar experience. I suppose she could see the pain and frustration in my face as I was still trying to analyze what went wrong. Finally, she looked at me and said, "You have to forgive yourself. There's nothing more to forgive him for. Forgive you."

And so I pass that advice along to you.

It Hurts Like Hell

The Maintain Stage is the hardest one to stick to, mostly because it's human nature to want what we can't have, and give into temptation, thinking, "just once won't hurt me." Yes, it will. It's like taking three steps forward and ten steps back. You don't go together because opposites don't always attract. Each time you let it happen, you end up further and further away from your goal. Think about all of the time and energy you've just put into rebuilding yourself this fabulous, amazing person. Why are you going to blow it on some schmuck who was dumb enough to dump your incredible ass in the first place? Save it for the next wonderful man you date who will actually appreciate you for everything you are, were, and will one day be. That is the only real regret that I have in these past few years... I'll never know what opportunities I may have passed up because I was too busy going through Stages 1-3 on repeat, like a cracked out junkie spinning a broken record.

Believe me, I know it's easier said that done. I am the queen of giving advice that I never take. It took making a lot of mistakes and learning the VERY hard way to finally get to the point where I could ignore his sporadic text messages and didn't go home in tears every time I would see him out. The best advice anyone could offer me was to stay away from him, which was not always an option. When I went to Costa Rica, I actually started looking for jobs out in California so I didn't have to return to the life we shared. Then I met this girl at a hostel who I ended up taking my first surf lesson with, and during a game of pool one afternoon, she said to me, "If you want to move to San Francisco because you want to move there, then do it. But if you are moving because you are running away from some guy, don't. Don't give him the satisfaction of determining your life and your choices. Go back to New York and live the life that's yours." She was right. And she said it in a fabulous British accent which made her that much cooler. Sometimes the best advice comes from the people who don't really know us at all. So I put on my big girl panties and decided no man was going to determine my happiness, my self-worth, or my place of habitation. I loved my life in New York. My family and friends were there, my grandparents were there, and my career was there. I had worked too hard to build relationships and a positive reputation in my community to just walk away from it all to start over again. It was time to stop running and start rebuilding.

I also had to finally acknowledge WHY I kept going back to him and change it. A year after we met, I closed my business of five years, picked up, moved to New York (where he was living), and started a whole new life. At twenty-seven years old, I was trying to make it as a writer after spending the first twenty-six years as a dancer and choreographer. But I was an "artist" and I embraced my community of poor, tortured souls with the same amount of self-loathing and desperate struggle as everyone else. I knew I had to find a job to pay the bills, but in this piss poor economy with nothing but a certification in Pilates and a smattering of teaching jobs on my resume, the task seemed impossible. Despite the fact that I owned a dance studio for five years and understood standard business fundamentals and practices, no one would hire me because I lacked "corporate" experience. Yet I couldn't build my resume without being someone's bitch, making barely enough money to cover my rent. Apparently running your own dance school at the age of twenty-three doesn't impress anyone in the rest of the business world. They would rather hire someone who's been getting coffee and designing PowerPoint presentations for the past four years.

Completely discouraged and feeling like an absolute failure, I turned to the only thing in my mind I could control, which was my relationship. I was NOT going to fail at that as well. The more and more I tried to fix us, the further he would push me away, coming back long enough to keep me hooked but maintaining enough distance that he didn't feel responsible for any of my feelings. We tortured each other's lives for that first year I lived in New York. We had grown so close at points and shared so much that it felt impossible to detach, but every time we made a go at it, our true intentions would be revealed (mine being that I wanted a real relationship and his being that he didn't love me) and we'd end up spitting violent words of hate at each other. Very healthy. So on top of being broke and incapable of holding a job for more than a few months, I had also buried myself deeply into an emotionally abusive relationship that I could not seem to tear myself away from. It's shocking that another man didn't swoop in to save me at the time; I must have been beaming with beauty, intelligence, and self-confidence. What's more shocking is that HE didn't realize how in love with me he was in those moments when we were hurling curse words, threats, pillows, and glares of disgust, amongst other things.

But I Miss Him...

Maintain may be the hardest, but it's also the most crucial stage of this shape up and ship out plan. As in all the other stages, you have to let it happen in your own time, but there are definitely little tips and hints to make it go quicker and smoother. The most important? Keep busy. Sit down and make a list of goals. What you want to accomplish today, this week, this month, over the next three months, by next year, by the time your next milestone birthday hits... you get the point. Make sure they are attainable but also somewhat challenging. Actually write them down, so that as you accomplish them, you can cross them off. That's my favorite part!

I am a huge fan of "To Do" lists, and the LIFE "To Do" list (also known as "The Bucket List") is by far the most important.

Next, sit down and write on a piece of loose-leaf paper everything you are looking for in a relationship. A very dear friend and mentor of mine gave me that suggestion, passed along to her by a friend who I'm sure read it in a self-help book somewhere along the way. After you write the list, tuck it away somewhere, and don't come back to it. She later told me that after she met her now-husband, she went back and found her list, and discovered that he had almost every quality that she listed on it. As "The Secret" says, if you put it out into the Universe, it will come back to you eventually. Or so everyone tells me. I haven't actually read it yet because I'm too busy juggling seven careers so I can make the 40 Under 40 List. The more people you share this book with, the better chances of that happening. No pressure.

Anyway. Don't cheat yourself… you deserve the best and should never settle for less. Let that list serve as a reminder, always. In fact, after you're married, you should have it framed.

Now that you've established what you DO want, it's time to finally put away the things you don't. In the Detox Stage, I discussed deleting his number and giving him back his belongings as quickly as possible, so theoretically you shouldn't have much left. Around the three year mark of our dysfunctional relationship, and the major fight that revealed I had been an asshole of epic proportions for wasting years of my love on this person, I angrily went home and ripped every item of clothing and crap that he had intentionally left at my apartment (because he'd been spending multiple nights per week there). The man literally had a section of his shit in my closet and had the NERVE to tell me that wasn't a "big deal." He had clothes everywhere. I now understand why women commit violent crimes that include castration, rat poison, and repeated stabbings.

So in a drama queen moment, I dumped a huge shopping bag of his shit at his place of work, thinking I had rid myself of everything. It felt good in the same way I would imagine an enema feels. That is until a few months later, when I was rearranging furniture in my apartment and came across a tie tucked behind my bed. Or when I was moving out and I found a small shopping bag with a pair of sweats and an old comfortable t-shirt of his that I had borrowed a few summers back and had pushed out of sight after one of our arguments. By the time I discovered I still had them, it was too late to give them back.

Another rule of Maintenance: Do not re-establish contact that will ignite any memory of the two of you as a couple. It only rips open the wound, and honestly, aren't you tired of throwing a Band-Aid on the same old cut? Let it heal and form the necessary scar.

When I returned home from Costa Rica in November 2010, I had given up my apartment in NYC and found those items lying in my closet at my parents' house. Why they made it through the move I'm not sure, but I guess subconsciously I wasn't really ready to completely let go. I folded them all up neatly in a bag and tucked them way on the top shelf next to the box of letters, cards, and dried corsages from previous ex-boyfriends. I'm sure one day I'll get rid of them completely. Right now, I have no desire to venture down Memory Lane, because that shit has not been paved in a few years and I'm bound to break an ankle.

It's OK to hold onto good memories. We are built, shaped, and molded by these experiences, and no one wants to spend their whole life looking back with hatred and anger on every relationship that doesn't work out. I don't necessarily agree with the whole "burn the bastard's sweaters in a bonfire in front of his apartment." Trust me, if you really want to hurt a man, go straight for the ego. Don't waste your time on his ugly sweater from 1998. The shirt didn't fuck another woman, he did.

However if you are still WEARING the clothes, stop. It's time to move on. Put down the recreational soccer T-shirt and return to your own wardrobe. Besides, baggy pants went out in the 90s. Show off that hot new body you've been working on with clothes that actually fit you.

Above all, look at how far you've come. A few years ago I was a different person. For better or for worse, that relationship changed me. My motivation to stay healthy and fit is no longer to win him back, but to lead a better life overall. While I am by no means old, I'm not getting any younger, and there are a lot of monumental things in my life waiting to happen. Do I need to be a supermodel when they happen? No. That ship sailed around middle school when I stopped growing vertically and starting growing hips. That doesn't mean I don't want to feel confident, happy and secure when I wake up in the morning and look in the mirror. I didn't feel those things for a long time, and sometimes I still don't. My last few relationships really knocked the self-esteem out of me. It takes a certain kind of person to be able to see someone you loved out with another woman and feel nothing, and I struggled with that, repeatedly.

Do this for YOU. The stages are designed to have slip-ups and mistakes. It's meant to reach the standard human being, with a broken heart and wounded soul. Be proud you have a heart and soul... A lot of people are lacking them these days. You are real, and you will make your way through all four stages in your own time. Also, you have to accept that you have a problem in the first place. Many people find it easy to point blame at the other person, never admitting fault or looking at the situation from another perspective. Typically, those are the same people who "fall off the wagon" over and over again in rehab, and end up picking up right where they left off. Here's something important for you to understand: I'm not telling you to change. YOU are the only person who has the power to determine if you need to change. YOU are the only person who knows what truly makes you happy. If you believe you needed this book in the first place, it should be because you have recognized a weakness or a flaw in yourself that you want to fix in order to avoid making the same mistakes in the future. While I have spoken extensively about this one particular relationship because of the amount of weight I lost during it, my patterns with romance and men have been the same throughout my twenties. In fact, I became painfully aware of this when I finally started dating again a few years back, and noticed I was still attracting the same kind of man.

I am living proof that even the most intelligent and driven woman can lose herself to a guy. I'm also living proof that in time, you will always come back to who you are and who

you are meant to be. And maybe even write
a book about it.

PART THREE:
ONE YEAR LATER...

Chapter Eight

For Real, This Time

"You can't start the next chapter of your life if you keep re-reading the last one." ~Unknown

As I mentioned in the first chapter, I wrote and completed this book in early 2011. I finished it, saved it, and never opened it again. I didn't share it with anyone, I didn't edit it, and I certainly didn't know what to do with it. Why?

I was ashamed. All that great advice and insight and wisdom I bestowed upon you? I didn't follow about 80% of it. I hit a wall, to be honest.

It started with Jack's relationship with a girl who was a client of his, whom he brought into everything—my work environment, my social environment, my circle of friends. I understood that these scenarios were part of his life as well, just as I understood it had been my choice to remain involved in a parallel life to his despite not being in the relationship I wanted. Nonetheless, it was awkward and uncomfortable, constantly. I hurt, constantly. I couldn't understand why he was so comfortable engaging in a very public, yet undefined, relationship with her when he never wanted ANYONE to know about me. I hated when my friends were nice to her. I felt alone and embarrassed, partly because of my behavior and partly because I knew he had trashed my name to his newfound "group" and completely denied the nature of our relationship in an effort to absolve himself of the sad and downright nasty things that had occurred in the last couple of years.

Look, I'm not a complete psycho, though I play the part well at times. I knew we weren't committed, and I knew that he was seeing other people. However, there are things you just don't do or say to or with a woman you don't truly love. And he broke all of those rules.

On top of that, last year I began working at a new fitness studio based in Tribeca. I thought this opportunity was going to be the break I needed—working in a new environment that had nothing to do with Jack, utilizing my fitness and business background to help launch a new company, plus have access to free classes to stay in shape. It seemed like a win all around, and the perfect solution to rebuild my new life while remaining in New York City.

About five months into working there, I approached the owner about taking on some classes to teach, in addition to my current roles of running the desk and managing the studio. Though there was really no clear "method" to what she was branding and selling, and most of the moves were just rip offs of other local studios where she had trained, I figured I had a decent grasp on what her concept was and I certainly was the most qualified to teach out of the rest of the staff, with my Pilates and dance background. Both her and the other owner, a male who shall also remain nameless, informed me that I did not have the right "look" to be teaching at the studio. He said they needed teachers in front of the room whom their fancy-pants Tribeca clients would want to look like. The male owner argued with me that if I trained hard enough I could essentially change my bone structure to have the same straight, boy-like figure of the other teachers, no matter how curvy I was. I found this fascinating, that he had discovered a fitness method that was capable of shaving away at bone mass, shrinking your skeletal remains to be on par with those of a twelve year old boy. This guy should really be the one writing a book right now. He's figured out a method that can only work through sprinkling fairy dust and defying all rules of modern medicine.

Needless to say, I walked out the door after that meeting and never looked back. There I was at twenty-nine years old, after years of battling body image disorders and excessively studying health, fitness and ways to maintain weight loss, and I was being told, essentially, that I was too fat to teach an exercise class.

So what did this dancer-writer-Pilates teacher-entrepreneur-of-something-that-was-yet-to-be-discovered, with no job, no love life, and no place to live because I had to relinquish yet another sublet until I knew how I'd be able to pay my bills do?

I booked a flight to London. And I planned a trip that would coincide with my art and music blog to go live in Europe for ten weeks. That's right. I ran. I left NYC, I left that bullshit excuse for a fitness studio, I left my twisted, no-longer-existent love life, and I set out to figure out what would make ME happy.

I lived in London and traveled through Europe for almost three months, and when I returned to New York things were different. The trip taught me how to stop running away from things, and instead how to run towards a semblance of a new life. Within two weeks of arriving home, I had clients in the business I was developing. I found a place to live. I still had a few battles to deal with in regards to my past relationship, but I was no longer going to be bullied into submission. I knew what happened between us, I knew where I went wrong but I wasn't taking the heat for his shortcomings and selfish tendencies. I stood my ground and refused a friendship and would not support his new girlfriend because when he was with her, he simply wasn't nice to me. I was done.

Then I made one crucial error and broke one of my own cardinal, steadfast rules — I became friends with a girl he dumped. DO NOT DO THIS. Repeat after me: I WILL NOT BECOME FRIENDS WITH ANY WOMAN MY EX IS OR HAS BEEN SLEEPING WITH. This rule is crucial to success in EVERY stage of this book. Why, you ask? Shouldn't I be all about "girl power" and scorned women of the world bonding together and ganging up against a scummy man? No. You shouldn't. This is not a movie and you will not end up best friends and future bridesmaids. You should let her figure it out on her own without dragging you down for the count.

Because here's what happens: You're out of the mess. You walked away. In time, you may even have a small chance at being friends/ civil with your ex, or at least pleasant acquaintances who can reminisce now and then about the few good memories you shared. (Maybe.) Suddenly, you have this woman in your ear reminding you about every ounce of pain you ever felt. Talking about how he broke her heart, and all the things he lied about, and how special she thought their relationship was. How YOU aren't crazy, because he did it to HER too! He's an emotional retard! He treats women like crap! You feel bad for her, and subconsciously try to save her in the way you were never able to save yourself. You open up and start sharing personal stories and painful memories. Slowly, the crazy unlocks and starts seeping into your veins and spreading throughout your body, like a virus you can't stop. You are pulled into the trenches of a battle you spent years trying to overcome, and you regret ever answering the bloody phone that day she called you crying.

THEN she decides to forgive him, starts spending all her free time with him, befriends all of your friends, his friends, his GIRLFRIEND, his family, and eventually sleeps with him again. And you realize it was ALL bullshit. You were part of a game, a pawn in her quest to obtain info to feed her obsession, a part of HER addiction. No bueno.

When I finally ended THAT situation—stopped being her "friend" and cut all communication with him and those romantically attached to him—then I was truly on the road to recovery. It was a dramatic move, but a necessary one. Last I heard, that former "friend" (who was calling me her "bestie" after two weeks of friendship) is still trying to "fix" him and he still hasn't changed. Regardless, that setback hurt me pretty bad and left a large and deep pool of resentment and damage that, well, I'm working on.

Major life lesson: Always trust your gut about people. If you ever feel uncomfortable and a tiny voice tells you something isn't right, listen to it. Always.

Though I feel sheepish admitting it, he was home to me for a long time, despite the horrendous conditions of our relationship for the majority of the years I knew him. I felt comfortable with him in a way I hadn't with most people over the course of my life. He was a part of my history, someone that knew me prior to my life in New York, one of the last of my adult friends who had supported my years as a dancer... and he was unfinished business. We never had an "official" committed relationship, where I could call him my "boyfriend" and really see what things could have been like between us. Maybe that's why I held on for so long. It wasn't a matter of letting go of the familiar... it was a matter of letting go of the unknown. I didn't want to be wrong. And you know what I learned? It's okay. It's okay to be wrong. You're going to continue to be wrong until you're right. It WAS a complete story. It just had a different ending than what I had scripted in my mind.

I realized, in seeing other relationships crumble around me, the desperation in which people attack love and the shaky foundations and superficial reasons people force it upon, that I don't mind being single right now. Someone once told me the only way to let the really great things find their way into your life is to drain out all the negative ones and be empty for a while. Sometimes, I still feel empty. So will you. But you'll find other outlets to challenge yourself and "fill" up as you continue growing into the person that you're supposed to be.

I turned thirty-one this past November, and so far, this decade is blowing the last one out of the water. My career is on a steady, uphill climb. I trained for and completed my first half marathon, I have strengthened relationships with all my family and friends (some of whom I isolated during those angry years), and I'm learning all about vitamins and skin care to help reverse the aging process without resorting to Botox. Apparently, you can still get acne in your thirties, which I find to be a cruel twist of nature. Perhaps that's why twenty-five year olds keep hitting on me... They see a monster zit on my chin and automatically assume those hideous whiteheads must clearly indicate I still check off the 18-24 box in most modern surveys. Thank you, Photoshop.

Maybe I'll be grow up to be a cougar. Women tend to outlive men anyway, so if I marry someone younger, based on statistics, I'll most likely end up dying around the same time as him, cutting off the pain of having to live without someone I love. Now that's true romance. Just like in "The Notebook." Who knows? The point is, it's exciting! I get to keep living, experiencing, meeting people and growing, without anyone telling me who I am or what I'm worth. And you know what else? When the right person comes along, I'll be ready. I'm not afraid anymore. Not of men, not of love, and not of complex carbohydrates and high-fructose products.

It may be one year later, but the method, inspiration, and meaning behind this book still holds true to form. Life is full of battles, whether they be of the heart, body or mind, and it is a personal choice to succumb to the demons or rise above and make changes. It all lies in your perception of control, your awareness of your triggers, and your level of self-respect. While you cannot control how you feel or situations in which someone or something might ignite a feeling of anger, sadness, or a sudden urge to binge eat Oreos, you can control the means in which you express and handle those feelings. This took me a LONG time to learn. I'm an extremist and a reactor. With food and exercise, I tend to either be full-force in "perfection mode" or I'm tired, depressed, lazy and unmotivated. With men, I'm the same. At this point in my life, one of my goals is to learn balance. Pace myself. Hit the gas pedal full force, every now and then throwing on cruise control and enjoying the scenery. Learning how to breathe and take it all in. Taking risks. Knowing that I can't control everything, but I'll never know if I don't try. Above all, I remember to respect myself. When my finger goes to the phone to text him, I stop and remember that I'm giving energy to someone who was not a good friend, lover, or overall human being toward me. Similarly to how I avoid mayo because it gives me an instant gag reflex. Respect your body, respect your mind. If you don't, how can you expect someone else to?

So if you think I'm a little crazy, you're probably right. I bet you are, too. That's why you're reading this, and then going to share it with all your friends via Facebook, Twitter, Pinterest, Tumblr, G-Chat and all other means of social media. Because at some point, probably around Stage One: Detox, you found yourself nodding in agreement and awkwardly looking toward the drawer where you buried his favorite high school football jersey and a bag of Peanut Butter M&Ms. And when you finish this book, the first thing you're going to do is sign on Facebook and defriend. (If you haven't already.)

No matter how crazy any of us are, deep down we're all human. We all can relate to each other. And we all have learned that forgiveness, moving on and letting go are three of the most difficult things to conquer in life.

With the thousands of friends you have on Facebook and in real life, trust me when I say you won't miss that one.

Defriend. And go spend time with the people that bring out the best version of you.

Above all, remember — you are never alone.

"Everything will be okay in the end. If it's not okay, it's not the end." ~Unknown

The End.

APPENDIX

Love the lists? Pin, Print and Post!

If you took nothing else away from this book, it should be that I'm obsessed with lists and believe that everyone else should be as well. (Actually, if that's all you took away then I have completely failed as a writer. Sorry.) We'll stay positive and go with the first option.

To make it easy for you to feed your new list obsession, I've put together this Appendix- a one-stop shop for all your OCD needs.

Here you'll find all of the "checklists" in the Detox, Repair and Strengthen stages ready to be ripped out, posted on your blog, or pinned to your Pinterest board. You can also find them on the DEFRIENDED website at www.defriendedthebook.com Make sure to hashtag #defriended when posting online to find other fantastic ladies to bond with over your newfound freedom, empowerment, and self-control.

You're welcome.

DEFRIENDED SUPERFOOD SHOPPING LIST

- ☐ Eggs
- ☐ Beans
- ☐ Greens
- ☐ Sweet Potatoes
- ☐ Salmon/Tuna
- ☐ Almonds/Walnuts
- ☐ Whole Grains
- ☐ Berries
- ☐ Yogurt
- ☐ Apples

DETOX STAGE   ~Rachel Albaum, RD, CDE

<u>Cell Phone Alias' for Your Ex</u>

Man Whore

Pathological Liar

Mind Fuck

Crazy Town

Heart Ache

Bad Idea

NO

DETOX STAGE   #DEFRIENDED

DE **138** FRIENDED

REPAIR Checklist

☐Get a haircut, color, or both.
☐Mani/pedi with the girls.
(Booze optional.)
☐Sign up for a class.
☐Plan a trip.
☐Volunteer.

REPAIR STAGE   #DEFRIENDED

REPAIR Rules

☐Variety is key.
☐Eat to live, don't live to eat.
☐Toss your "fat" clothes.
☐Get moving.
☐Stop when you're full.
☐Throw it out.
☐Fat is your friend.

REPAIR STAGE   #DEFRIENDED

Healthy Alternatives That Won't Break The Bank or the Belly

☐ *Jamba Juice-* Acai Super Antioxidant, 16 oz.: 260 calories.

☐ *Starbucks-* Tall Nonfat Latte: 90 calories, Spinach, Roasted Tomato, Feta, and Egg White Wrap: 280 calories

☐ *Qdoba Mexican Grill-* Grilled Veggie Burrito, Naked, with black beans, cheese, and pico de gallo: 380 calories

☐ *Dunkin Donuts-* Medium Coffee with Skim Milk and Splenda: 30 calories, Multigrain Bagel: 390 calories, with reduced fat cream cheese.

☐ *Whole Foods Sushi-* Avocado cucumber roll: 158 calories, Brown rice California roll: 177 calories, Brown rice Spicy Tuna Avocado roll: 189 calories, Rainbow roll: 186 calories, Spicy Shrimp Tempura roll: 193 calories, Edamame: 50 calories.

☐ *Panera Bread-* You Pick Two- Low-Fat Vegetarian Black Bean Soup: 170 calories, Half Asian Sesame Chicken Salad: 200 calories.

☐ *Au Bon Pain-* Turkey and Swiss on a Farmhouse Roll (Half Sandwich): 320 calories, Medium Diet Pepsi: 0 calories, Small Fruit Cup: 70 calories.

REPAIR STAGE   #DEFRIENDED

STRENGTHEN Starters

☐Lay it out the night before.
☐Take advantage of your
lunch break.
☐Plan it around your favorite
TV show.

STRENGTHEN STAGE   #DEFRIENDED

Savvy Strengthening-Mix and Match!

Ab-tastic
- [ ] The Hundred
- [ ] The Plank
- [ ] The Scissor
- [ ] The Reverse Curl

"Armed" and Dangerous
- [ ] 7/7/7
- [ ] Tricep Dips
- [ ] Push Ups
- [ ] Sculpted Shoulders

Bootylicious
- [ ] Ballerina Squat
- [ ] Standard Squat
- [ ] Can Can
- [ ] Butt Lift

Break a Sweat
- [ ] Workout DVD's/OnDemand
- [ ] Child Play
- [ ] Hit the Pavement
- [ ] No More Couch Potato
- [ ] Killer Classes

STRENGTHEN STAGE   #DEFRIENDED

DE **148** FRIENDED

Be a "Class Act"

☐Anti-Gravity Yoga

☐Boot Camp

☐Pole Dancing

☐Pilates

☐Bikram Yoga

☐Hip Hop

☐Spinning

☐Self-Defense

☐Ballet

☐Meditation

☐Boot Camp

☐Kickboxing

☐Running groups

☐Real Boxing

STRENGTHEN STAGE   #DEFRIENDED

READERS CHOICE
Playlist: *Ultimate Break Up*

- Toni Braxton, "Breathe Again"
- Natasha Bedingfield, "Happy"
- John Mayer, "Slow Dancing In a Burning Room"
- Tony Rich Project, "Nobody Knows"
- Rachel Yamagata, "Reasons Why"
- Rascal Flatts, "What Hurts The Most"
- Joanna Newsom, "On a Good Day"
- Evanescence, "Everybody's Fool"
- Lifehouse, "Broken"
- Donna Summer, "I Will Survive"
- Cee Lo, "Fuck You"
- Three Days Grace, "I Hate Everything About You"
- Sara Bareilles, "Basket Case"
- Coldplay, "The Hardest Part"
- OAR, "Shattered"
- Pearl Jam, "Come Back"
- Christina Aguilera, "Fighter"
- Carrie Underwood, "Before He Cheats"
- Sugarland, "Settlin"
- Jewel, "Please Don't Say I Love You"

STRENGTHEN STAGE   #DEFRIENDED

DE **152** FRIENDED

CHRISTINA'S CHOICE
Playlist: *You Just Need a Good Cry*

‣Bonnie Raitt, "I Can't Make You Love Me"
‣James Morrison, "The Pieces Don't Fit Anymore"
‣The Civil Wars, "Poison and Wine"
‣Barnaby Bright, "Made Up Of"
‣Tracy Chapman, "Smoke and Ashes"
‣Missy Higgins, "Where I Stood"
‣Annie Lennox, "Waiting In Vain"
‣Randy Newman, "Feels Like Home"
‣Anna Krantz, "Rubble and the Dust"
‣Patty Griffin, "Let Him Fly"
‣David Gray, "Say Hello, Wave Goodbye"
‣Carole King, "Will You Still Love Me Tomorrow"
‣Martin Rivas, "Get Yourself Together"
‣Amos Lee, "Learned A Lot"
‣Adele, "Someone Like You"
‣Bill Withers, "Ain't No Sunshine"
‣Brandi Carlile, "That Wasn't Me"
‣Madi Diaz, "A Little Bit"
‣Jeff Buckley, "Lover, You Should Have Come Over"
‣Fleetwood Mac, "Landslide"

STRENGTHEN STAGE   #DEFRIENDED

DE **154** FRIENDED

CHRISTINA'S CHOICE
Playlist: *Motivation*

‣Alanis Morissette, "You Oughta Know"
‣Fun., "Some Nights"
‣Adele, "Rumour Has It"
‣Aerosmith, "Cryin' "
‣Will Hoge, "Better Off Now (That You're Gone)"
‣James Morrison, "Nothing Ever Hurt Like You"
‣Kelly Clarkson, "Since You've Been Gone"
‣Daughtry, "Over You"
‣One Republic, "Good Life"
‣Taylor Swift, "We Are Never Getting Back Together"
‣Sara Bareilles, "Let the Rain"
‣The Lumineers, "Classy Girls"
‣Florence and the Machine, "Dog Days Are Over"
‣Eminem, "Love the Way You Lie"
‣Natasha Bedingfield, "Unwritten"
‣Justin Timberlake, "Cry Me a River"
‣Dixie Chicks, "Not Ready To Make Nice"
‣Destiny's Child, "Survivor"
‣Pink, "Blow Me (One Last Kiss)"
‣Katy Perry, "Wide Awake"
‣U2, "Still Haven't Found What I'm Looking For"

STRENGTHEN STAGE   #DEFRIENDED

DE **156** FRIENDED

Acknowledgements

To Diana Hershberger, Kasey Williams, Samantha Hawley, Lauren Chapman, Ree Merrill, Bri Arden, Elizabeth Boyle, Chrissi Poland, Andrea Normandia, Becky Bliss, Maggie McGill, my CEO artists Anna Krantz, Meaghan Farrell and Ariel Lask, everyone who participated in the DEFRIENDED survey, and all the amazing women I've known throughout my life- for the tears, the laughter, the advice, the tough love, the patience, the drinks, the dancing, the e-mails, texts and calls, the heart-to-hearts, the ladies nights, the bad dates, the broken hearts, all the firsts and all the lasts. You loved me even when I didn't love me, and you've shown ME that I'm never truly alone. I love you all.

To JeanMarie Romanella and Nicole Romanella, my "little sisters", my heart, my toughest critics and my most loyal supporters. No ex-boyfriend, ex-husband, or ex-friend-with-benefits could ever come between the bond that we share. And Nicole, thank you for that one warm spring night in May. It brought me to exactly where I needed to be.

To Rocky Romanella, Andrew Romanella, Justin Albaum, Gaetano D'Andrea, Caleb Hawley, Tommy Merrill, Sean O'Neal and all the other men in my life who gave me frank and sometimes painful insight into the male brain, and for loving me despite my crazy female brain.

To my family and "fra-mily"- Aunt Debbie, Uncle Rocky, Emy, Tony, Ali, Kim, Aunt Luann, Uncle Peter, Katie, Aunt MaryAnn, Uncle Joey, Uncle Anthony- who came to every "going away" party, supported every new career, brought housewarming gifts to all my new apartments, and still managed to figure out how to send me birthday and Christmas gifts even when you had no idea where the hell I was living at the time.

To Martin Rivas, not only for designing a beautiful cover, but for being one of my first friends in New York City. Your beautiful music, generous heart and warm energy are unparalleled. And Patti Rivas, for your unexpected thoughtfulness and quiet encouragement. That is one lucky kid.

To Rachel Albaum, for contributing your health and well-being wisdom to the Detox Stage of this book.

To Grandma Marie, Grandpa Tony, Grandma Tuddy and Grandpa Champ. I am a better person for having known all of you, and for having a piece of each of you to carry with me wherever I go.

To my brother Anthony Morelli, for reading everything I've ever written and quoting back your favorite lines. For marking my climb up the celebrity letter list. Through all the laughter, all the late night talks, and all the "Why are you still talking to him?" lectures... You're the reason I know good guys still exist.

To my dad, Fred Morelli, the man who instilled the importance of being your own boss, doing what you love, treating life like an adventure, and never settling for second best. More importantly, for always trying to understand what exactly it is I do for a living, and for always having "small bills" while I was figuring it out myself.

To my mom, Donna Morelli, for teaching me how to read, how to write, how to love and how to forgive. For thinking I'm the most beautiful girl in the world even when I couldn't bear to look in a mirror and for staying calm through the countless meltdowns of my teens and 20s (okay, of my whole life). Most of all, for believing this book was going to be a huge success without ever having read a word of it.

To every person who gave me a couch to sleep on, a room to sublet, a contact to meet in a city I'd never been, advice for the road, advice on life, a hot meal, a free drink, an ear to listen and a reason to still believe. I could never have pursued my dream to be a writer without the colorful characters who filled my life with experience, memories and a past exciting enough to pass along.

And finally, to every guy who broke my heart, every person who called me fat, all those who called me crazy, and all those who stopped calling me for no rhyme or reason whatsoever.

I thank you most of all.

About the Author

Christina Morelli is a freelance writer temporarily living in New York City until her next adventure. Other professions include but are not limited to artist manager, marketing director, social media guru, dance instructor, choreographer, Pilates trainer, psychology teacher, photographer, editor, receptionist, blogger, ghost writer, journalist, philanthropist, dolphin trainer, and professional traveler.*

Christina has written for various independent music magazines, business websites, professional blogs, and personal publications, in addition to serving as editor-in-chief for NYC Art Scene. In 2011 she founded The CEO Artist, an artist development, marketing and management company based in NYC.

For Christina's professional work, please visit www.theceoartist.com.

For Christina's running social commentary on life, love and NYC, inspirational photos, and various other pearls of wisdom please visit www.christinamorelli.com.

One of these professions is false. But it's on her bucket list.

Stalk Me, Not Him

Website
www.christinamorelli.com
www.defriendedthebook.com

Twitter
www.twitter.com/cmorellinyc
www.twitter.com/defriendedbook

Facebook
www.facebook.com/
defriendedthebook

Instagram
www.instagram.com/cmorellinyc